TREASURE TROVE

TREASURE TROVE

Where to Find the Great Lost Treasures of the World

Tim Haydock

Fourth Estate · London

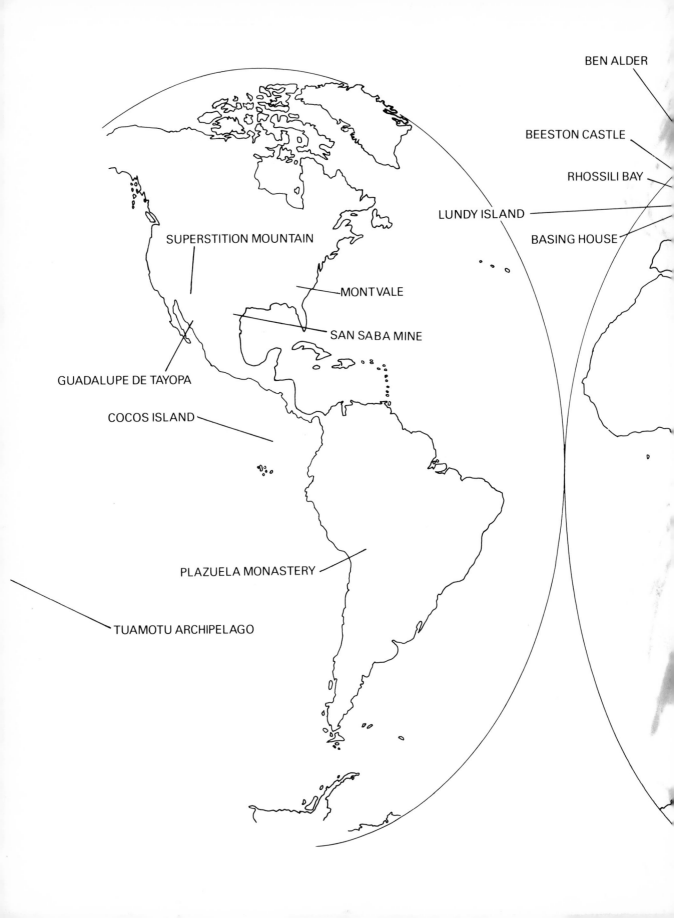

BEN ALDER

BEESTON CASTLE

RHOSSILI BAY

LUNDY ISLAND

BASING HOUSE

SUPERSTITION MOUNTAIN

MONTVALE

SAN SABA MINE

GUADALUPE DE TAYOPA

COCOS ISLAND

PLAZUELA MONASTERY

TUAMOTU ARCHIPELAGO

H21 700 336 7   HAYDOCK, T.
                 Treasure trove
                                    £9.95

910.4'53

-9 OCT. 1986

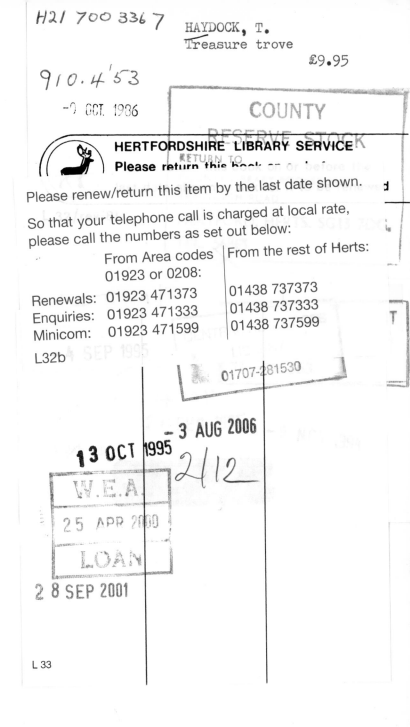

FAST CASTLE

RENNES-LE-CHÂTEAU

AGRIHAN

Designed and produced by
Breslich & Foss
Golden House
28–31 Great Pulteney Street
London W1R 3DD

Editor: Nicholas Robinson
Editorial Consultant: Mark Daniel
Assistant Editor: Annabel Edwards
Map Research: Gavin Ingham Brooke
Designer: Harold Bartram

First published in Great Britain by
Fourth Estate Ltd
Classic House
113 Westbourne Grove
London W2 4UP

British Library Cataloguing in Publication Data

Haydock, Tim
    Treasure trove : where to find the great
    lost treasures of the world.
    1. Treasure-trove
    I. Title
    910.4'53   G525
    ISBN 0–947795–30–8

Photoset by Fakenham Photosetting Ltd, Fakenham, Norfolk.
Printed and bound in Great Britain by The Bath Press, Avon.

CONTENTS

To my Mother with love

AUTHOR'S ACKNOWLEDGEMENTS

For a work of this kind an author's obligations are wide-ranging, and I am bound to acknowledge the kind assistance of many more than I am able to name here.

To the staff of the Bodleian Library, the staff of the British Library and especially of the Map Room, always most courteous and helpful, I offer my particular thanks. To Roy Norvill, the Hon. Christopher Orde-Powlett and Tatiana Kletzky-Pradère who gave most freely of their time in reply to enquiries; to Peter Stewart, John Howland, Tony Morrison and Mark Howell; to John Mussell and Mick Turrell of *The Searcher* Magazine, Surrey, and John Bowman of the Ancient Britain Research Society, I am grateful for a wide variety of specialist knowledge. To Pamela Trill, my typist; to Michèle Wooldridge for help with translation; to my brother, Jonathan, for most helpful suggestions and source material; to Jonas and Joelle Pettersson for a tiresome guest well looked after; to Gavin Ingham Brooke for help with translation and masterminding the maps; to Annabel Edwards for trouble-shooting and tracking down invaluable information; to Mark Daniel for a fresh and thoughtful point of view and incalculable improvements to the text; to his wife, Anne, who gave much needed assistance at a late and vital stage; to Nicholas Robinson for benefits received more than he well can know; and to Sally Berner for unfailing inspiration but still no scrambled egg; to all of these my warmest gratitude and appreciation.

ILLUSTRATION ACKNOWLEDGEMENTS

Breslich & Foss would like to thank all the museums, art galleries, photographic libraries, agencies, and private individuals who provided photographs for this book. Acknowledgements are due as follows:

The Mansell Collection page 13, Tourism Commission, New South Wales 16–17, Peter Newark's Western Americana 20, 22, 76, 79 (left), 126, 127, 136, 137, Marion & Tony Morrison South American Pictures 24, 25, 100–101, 102, 106 (left & right), John Bowman 28, Topham 31, 40, The J. Allan Cash Photolibrary 41, 46, National Portrait Gallery, London 43, 70, 120, Mary Evans Picture Library 47, 50, K. M. Andrew 52, Photo-Centre, Berwick 71, R. Cooper, Lundy Public Relations 86, Jones Memorial Library, Lynchburg, Va. 89, James Davis Library 93, Louvre, Paris 120, Wales Tourist Board 122.

INTRODUCTION

Any author presumptuous enough to discuss the sites of lost treasure runs the risk of having his work read with a sceptical eye and a wry smile. What better excuse, after all, can there be for a good yarn? Stories of undiscovered treasure are frequently a mixture of hearsay, romance and wishful thinking. Nonetheless, year after year reports of successful discoveries make the headlines, and the treasure hunters' magazines are filled every month with accounts of small finds.

The idea behind the choice of sites suggested in this book is that while very few people have the resources or inclination to embark upon the exploration of the great marine wrecks, they are quite capable, thanks in part to the development of the metal detector, of searching with some hope of success for landbased finds. The most successful of the professional metal detector users, or metal detectorists as they are called, manage to make a living from what is essentially a hobby by virtue of painstaking research and perseverance in the field. However, the individual treasure hunter is normally restricted to the chance discovery of small hoards which may, at most, yield a few thousand pounds or dollars. The great discoveries seem to be beyond him.

On the other hand, the libraries of the world are full of books of stories of missing treasures written in such a way that the reader feels it is simply a matter of turning up on the spot with a shovel. The truth of the matter is that amidst the tall tales and tantalizing myths, there are a few stories for which the documents, historical circumstances and sometimes previous searches indicate that further investigation might bear fruit for the individual or small group. The contents of this book cannot and will not, on their own, lead the reader directly to wealth beyond his wildest dreams. If anyone believes they will, then it is only too easy to point out that I have my own shovel, so to speak.

This book is intended to be a starting point, based on historical research after careful consideration of much material. Some of the entries deal with the most famous treasure stories in the world—Rennes-le-Château, Cocos Island and Montvale. These are stories which have been written about endlessly, but for different reasons each seems to contain enough indications of missing—and in the first two cases partially recovered—wealth in a particular location that I have thought them worth including. Others, such as Agrihan and Rhossili Bay have slim sources but satisfy the criteria of sound historical basis and a possible site. Each entry in turn represents a puzzle and in most cases common sense will tell the reader that he must satisfy himself as to its likely solution before setting out in search of the treasure itself.

An interesting approach is to dowse the maps of possible sites. Mineral and water dowsing with rods is now an accepted method of locating hidden resources, but maps have also been dowsed successfully. John Bowman, a leading dowser, tested some of the maps in this book with a pendulum and has suggested several sites, most notably the hoards at Rhossili and Agrihan. He pinpointed the latter correctly amongst all the islands of the Mariana group.

The text does not go into the practical details of metal detecting, geological surveying or any of the other skills required to extract objects from the ground. These are all fully covered in other books. It is important, though, that the reader realizes the care and attention which must be taken if he is not to break the law. Almost all countries now have protected their archaeological sites by legislation and all have strict laws relating to treasure hunting and the discovery of buried treasure. In English law, articles of gold or silver may be declared treasure trove if, in the local coroner's view, the original owner hid them with the intention of returning later to reclaim them. In many countries, including Scotland, the law covers ancient finds in any material.

Finds of gold and silver in England, Wales and Northern Ireland, therefore, must be reported. In practice this serves to protect the finder who will be recompensed the full market value of the treasure if it is declared treasure trove and a local museum or the Crown decide to retain it. In many cases, however, the find is merely returned to the finder who then owns it legally. If the find, on the other hand, is not reported it is not regarded as the property of the finder who may be severely penalized if he is discovered. Unreported finds, whether declared treasure trove or not, will certainly be confiscated. It is worth remembering that more than £600,000 has been paid to finders of treasure trove in the United Kingdom since the Treasure Trove Review Committee was established in 1977.

In the United States the laws regarding the finding of treasure are State and not Federal laws, so it is necessary to check for each state. The general principle, however, is akin to that of lost property and the finder has superior rights to the treasure over everyone except the original owner and his heirs.

In comparison, the English laws covering treasure seeking may seem severe for they limit the scope of the individual searcher. In fact, they are both reasonable and fair. In a small country land always belongs to someone and cannot be trespassed and dug upon at will, nor can objects in the ground on someone else's property be removed any more legally than those on top of it. Therefore, the cardinal rule before starting work anywhere is to ask permission.

The National Council for Metal Detecting in Great Britain has issued a thoroughly sensible and practical code of conduct for detector users and it applies just as well to those seeking treasure by any other means and in other countries. The relevant passages are:

1. Do not trespass. Ask permission before venturing on to any private land.

2. Respect the Country Code. Do not leave gates open when crossing fields, and do not damage crops or frighten animals.

3. Do not leave a mess. It is perfectly simple to extract a coin or other small object buried a few inches under the ground without digging a great hole. Use a sharpened trowel or knife to cut a neat flap (do not remove the plug of earth entirely from the ground), extract the object, replace the soil and grass carefully and even you will have difficulty in finding the spot again.

4. Help to keep Britain tidy—and help yourself. Bottle tops, silver paper and tin cans are the last things you should throw away. You could well be digging them up again next year. Do yourself and the community a favour by taking the rusty iron and junk you find to the nearest litter bin.

5. If you discover any live ammunition or any lethal object such as an unexploded bomb or mine, do not touch it. Mark the site carefully and report the find to the local police and landowner.

6. Report all unusual historical finds to the landowner.

7. Familiarize yourself with the law relating to archaeological sites. Remember it is illegal for anyone to use a metal detector on a scheduled ancient monument unless permission has been

John Bowman map dowsing.

obtained from the Secretary of State for the Environment. Also acquaint yourself with the practice of Treasure Trove.

Parts 6 and 7 of the code introduce the most controversial area of treasure hunting—interference with archaeology. Over the years archaeologists have come to view treasure hunters, and metal detectorists in particular, with grave suspicion. Much of the problem has been brought about by the occasional looting of important sites and, more commonly, the failure of searchers to realize that years of painstaking research by archaeologists can be destroyed in a few minutes if any object is moved even a few inches in the ground, let alone taken away.

Potential treasure seekers should understand that they have as much, if not more, to learn from archaeology than vice versa. As a discipline it has, in the last few decades, added immeasurably to our understanding of the past and to our knowledge of where and how future discoveries may be made. As a branch of historical study it provides sound and detailed research into the past, and while this will not satisfy the treasure hunter as an end in itself, it is the only starting point from which he can have any realistic hope of success.

WORLD TREASURE STORIES— FACT AND FICTION

Treasure-hunting, like betting, has acquired a bad name. No matter that much of the economy is founded upon treasure-hunting and betting—for what else are oil or mineral speculation and investment in the stock market?—the treasure-hunter is too often seen as no more than an obsessive dreamer, the professional gambler as a rogue, while the investor or the broker is regarded as staid and unadventurous. The one view is as misguided as the other. There have been many mad treasure-hunters and many reckless punters, just as there have been many dull businessmen, but theirs are not generally the success stories.

Treasure-hunting, like serious betting, entails a lot of hard work, some luck and an intelligent degree of investment. Like betting, it can be dangerous. Many of the heroes and villains of this book have become addicted to their pursuits. Often, as with the compulsive gambler, an interest which started in innocent avarice becomes an end in itself. The pursuit comes to matter more than the quarry. It has destroyed families and friendships, made paupers of rich men and, very occasionally, rich men of paupers. There is much buried treasure in the world, but the man with a metal detector on, say, Superstition Mountain realizes just how big the world is when every square foot must be covered.

There are successful treasure-hunters, just as there are successful gamblers. Their principles are the same.

First, the 'natural' treasure-hunter, like the 'natural' gambler, should not do what comes naturally. Over-enthusiasm, credulity and the reckless readiness to risk everything on one throw of the dice are not temperamental qualities to be commended. Those who take chances by nature should not dwell in a world governed by chance. The professional gambler works hard in his study, following the old military principle that 'time spent in reconnaissance is seldom wasted'. Only when he has minimized all elements of risk does he commit himself. The professional gambler is as certain of his odds of success as the stockbroker. The treasure-hunter should also be so.

Second, the hunter must know when to cut his losses. This book is full of stories of men who did not know when to give up. A given amount of time and money spent in treasure-hunting should be regarded as well spent whether the treasure is found or not.

Third, the treasure-hunter invests only what he can afford. There is no need to spend fortunes and many years in pursuit of a treasure. It can almost be regarded, indeed as a recipe for disaster to do so. The Emperor Nero was lured by the words of some Carthaginian dreamer to mount a huge expedition into Africa in 65 A.D. to search for 'the gold of Dido' said to be buried in a deep cave. Nero was almost bankrupt when the expedition set out, but the idea of limitless wealth made him empty his coffers in a fruitless search. Reginald Cruise-Wilkins spent twenty-nine years on Mahé, in the Seychelles, attempting to associate some vague scratchings on the rocks of Bel Ombre beach with the legendary treasure codes of two pirates, Le Vasseur and Nageon de l'Estang, who were not even known to have visited Mahé and whose wealth may well have been mythical. With each disappointment, he sought and of course found some new possible explanation, working backwards, as it were, from hypothesis to proof.

This illustrates another principle followed by

successful gamblers and treasure-hunters. They always play the cards, that is, they do not increase their stake simply because they are frustrated at not having won a hand for a while. The cards— the evidence—are all that can guide the treasure-hunter and justify further speculation. If the evidence is insufficient, he gives up. If it is good, he continues.

Tradition is at once the hunter's friend and his bitterest enemy. It is in the nature of treasure stories that they are exaggerated and distorted in the retelling. There are notable cases of traditions so old that they have been disregarded yet which after careful and sceptical sifting, have proved to contain a grain of truth. An old Celtic ballad led two Irish speculators to treasure in the 1680s. They first heard the ballad sung by a harper near Ballyshannon:

> In earth beside the loud cascade,
> The son of Sora's king we laid,
> And on each finger placed a ring
> Of gold by mandate of the king.

They understood the waterfall to be the 'Salmon's Leap' at Ballyshannon and searched at the site. They discovered two gold plates, one of which is now in the Ashmolean museum at Oxford, dating from the eighth or ninth century.

Money may be the root of all evil, but it may also be claimed that evil is the source of all treasure. The treasure seeker does not keep exalted company. Everywhere he deals with treachery, oppression, looting and murder.

Death, fear and crime: these are the reasons for committing to the ground what might otherwise ease the lot of the living. For as long as men have buried their dead, it seems, they have sought to honour them, protect them or speed them on their journey to the shadows by laying precious artefacts in their tombs.

Treasures of the Tomb

The tombs of the Pharaohs, of Tutankhamun and of Nefertiti, the extraordinary Mount Li, burial site of Emperor Ch'in Shih Huang-ti, guarded by six thousand life-sized terracotta figures and one

In 1948, Reginald Cruise-Wilkins came to Mahé in the Seychelles to convalesce after a bout of malaria. Following a meeting with a Norwegian who owned a cryptogram, he was to spend the remainder of his life in vain pursuit of a pirate treasure that was believed to be hidden on one of the island's beaches.

hundred horse-drawn chariots, the solid jade armour of Prince Lin Sheng and his wife Tou Wan, the staggering wealth of the ship burial at Sutton Hoo—all these are well known, but many thousands of lesser kings, emperors, noblemen and commoners have been buried with their treasures and lie yet undisturbed.

The ancient custom has not died out. Nor, alas, has the equally pervasive crime of grave robbery. Rameses IX (B.C. 1142–23) drew up a set of papyri relating to the prosecution of grave robbers. Thracian, Etruscan, Scythian and Chinese tombs were often looted almost as soon as they were closed. In ancient Greece, *tymborychoi* broke into the graves of barely cold patricians. In Italy today full-time professional *tomboroli* exist, frequently men of immense skill and considerable historical and archaeological erudition. Occasionally they are caught and prosecuted. For the most part they thrive, for what is a museum curator or a collector to do when offered some rare and valuable collection which he suspects, but cannot prove, has been removed from a tomb? If he refuses to buy it, it is likely that it will be dispersed or even melted down. If he does not, he is accessory to a crime.

Alaric, King of the Visigoths

The ethical line between archaeology and grave-robbery is at times difficult to draw, but there are some legendary undiscovered tombs so ancient that the search for them must be regarded as fair game by any save the most obsessive of puritans. Notable amongst these is the grave of Alaric, King of the Visigoths. After sacking Rome, he led his train, laden with booty, southwards towards Sicily and Africa. In A.D. 410, still under thirty-five, he died at Cosenza in Calabria.

According to legend, he was buried in the bed of the River Busento. Calabrian prisoners were ordered temporarily to divert the river's course. When Alaric had been buried, mounted upon his favourite horse and surrounded by an enormous

Alaric, king of the Visigoths (portrayed here in a romanticized nineteenth-century engraving), died suddenly in 410 A.D. after sacking Rome. He was buried in the bed of the River Busento, surrounded by his vast treasure.

hoard of booty, the original banks of the river were reconstructed and the prisoners who had done the work were put to the sword. Beneath the Busento, therefore, sits Alaric with, so it is said, 25 tons of gold and 150 tons of silver.

We need not believe that the Visigoths would have left quite so enormous a hoard as that. Such hyperbole is commonplace in stories of treasure. We can reasonably, however, believe that the legend is derived from fact, that Alaric would have been buried with honour and with substantial wealth and even that his troops would have gone to such lengths to keep his tomb inviolate.

The Italian government is reluctant to grant concessions to treasure hunters, but many searches have been made. In 1965, a spot was identified near Cosenza where the river had actually been diverted many centuries before.

Genghis Khan

The area of search for the tomb of another great war lord, Genghis Khan, is very much wider. The great Mongolian chieftain died in a riding accident on 18 August or 24 August 1227. He was well over sixty. An enormous cortège is said to have accompanied his body back from Ning Hsia, the capital of Tanguten, to his burial place. Those who saw the procession were put to death, both in order to appease the gods and, more immediately, to prevent the news of his death from reaching his homeland before his sons could secure the succession.

There are two traditions relating to the burial site, but the legend as to the manner of that burial is consistent. The Khan was laid in a coffin of silver which rested in turn on the seventy-eight crowns of the rulers whom he had defeated. His weapons were laid close by him, as were a life-sized jade tiger, a lion, a horse and a manuscript Bible by an English monk. This rather charming inventory rings strangely true. It is not overblown like that of Alaric's tomb. Somehow these votive tributes accord well with the idea of the devout, ruthless, practical professional commander.

Some claim that this grave lies close to the scene of the Khan's fatal accident, beneath a mighty tree which stood on the summit of Mount Burkan Kaldun near Tangut. Ten thousand horsemen rode over the grave to obliterate all sign of its whereabouts. Soon saplings grew from the one great tree and the tomb was covered by impenetrable forest. We know the range, Bejun-Boldok, in which this mountain stands, but we have no idea which peak can be identified as Burkan Kaldun.

The other legend has it that the body was brought back to Ordos, in South Eastern Inner Mongolia. Eight identical tents containing identical coffins and relics were placed in the Kentei Mountains, in Altai, on Burkan Kaldun and in Ordos, in order to confuse those who might seek the grave. In the smaller tents were the relics, in the principal one the silver coffin. The precise location of three of these sites has been lost, but the eight white tents in Ordos, referred to as the 'Palace of Genghis Khan' were known, it is claimed, until the outbreak of the Second World War. Ordos Mongolian families still honour Genghis Khan and some even bear titles such as 'overseer of horse and weapons' which date back to the days of the Khan's great empire.

Treasure Hidden from Fear

The commonest motive for hiding wealth is fear, usually excited by social upheaval—war, revolution and exile. Most of the Viking, Celtic, Saxon and Roman hoards found in Britain, for example, were buried as invading powers approached. Some are enormous and represent the wealth of whole communities, of noblemen or of usurers. Some consist in a few coins or trinkets hastily hidden in a garden or in a courtyard.

The French Revolution, in that it was devastating and relatively recent, has spawned a host of similar tales. Some may have been invented by resentful revolutionaries, but many must be true. Madame du Barry, for example, formerly Louis XV's mistress, possessed an enormous number of jewels and other valuables bestowed upon her by her royal lover. Although she had retired to her estate near Sceaux on the death of the old king, her close association with the court and her bids to help her old friends were sufficient to condemn her. Shortly before her arrest, she buried both her money and her jewels in and around her château. She went to the guillotine on 7 December 1793. Only a few of her treasures were found. One and a half million *livres d'or* were also buried at this time somewhere in the Château de Bourdeilles in the Dordogne. At Villeneuve-lès-Avignon, formerly the anti-pope's summer palace on the opposite bank of the Rhône from the city, the Carthusian monks—who must indeed have had enormous wealth—buried their church plate, reliquaries and money in several spots indicated in some way by the boundary stones. The priory is now in ruins, but in 1957, the curator received some information which made him strip the panelling from one inner wall. He found engraved in the stone a plan including symbols and figures which have yet to be satisfactorily interpreted.

Fear caused Major General Edward Braddock to hide his troops' pay chest in 1775. Braddock was commanding a British Force against the French and Indian rebels based at Fort Duquesne (now Pittsburgh). On the long march from Fort Cumberland, he stopped one night at Frederick in Maryland. Afraid that it would slow down his troops and might fall into enemy hands, he decided to hide the pay chest before heading westward into the interior. With one trusted trooper, he climbed the hill behind the town and buried the chest. A few days later, his force was decimated at Monongahela river. Braddock himself was killed. A whole campaign payroll for 1,200 men lies buried somewhere on that hill which is nowadays known as Braddock Heights.

A similar story concerns Lord Howe island in the Tasman sea. The brig *George* moored there to take on water in 1830. Her commander was Captain Rattenbury. The *George* had already completed one successful whaling expedition that year. The oil had been sold in Sydney for cash and Rattenbury and his crew had sailed northward in search of more whales with five thousand sovereigns stored in the hold.

As Rattenbury waited for the boat with the water casks to return to the ship, a thick fog descended and the *George* was severely holed by a rock which now bears her name. Rattenbury was an experienced sailor. He contrived to beach her on the shore and unloaded the money and some provisions. The castaways did not know that the island was uninhabited. For fear of savage natives,

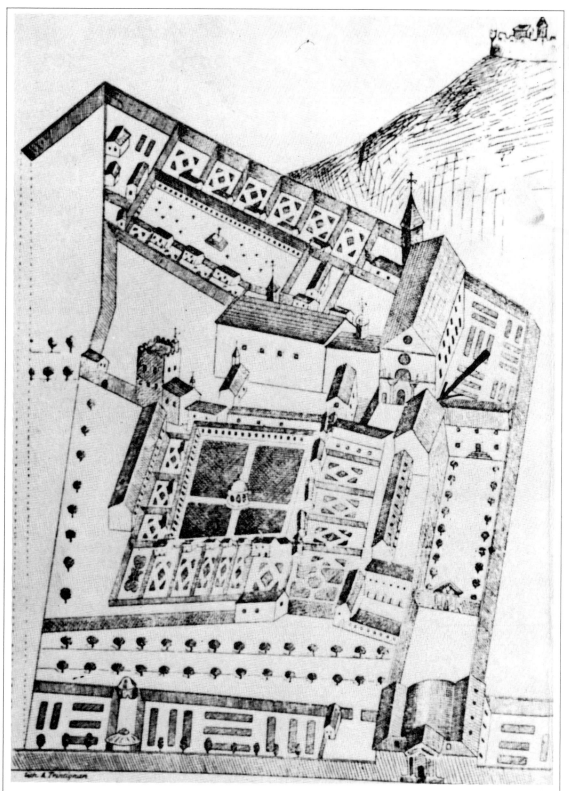

The Carthusian monastery at Villeneuve-lès-Avignon is said to conceal a treasure hidden during the French Revolution. The arrow may mark the entrance to the underground passage where it lies.

Lord Howe Island, lying off the coast of eastern Australia in the Tasman Sea, was visited in 1830 by the brig *George* under her commander, Captain Rattenbury. The vessel was holed by a rock and the captain unloaded part of the ship's provisions, including 5,000 sovereigns, which were buried for safekeeping. Rattenbury and his men made no

therefore, Rattenbury buried the sovereigns and he and his crew stayed close to the shore.

When, shortly afterwards, they were rescued by the *Elizabeth* and the *Nelson*, Rattenbury made no mention of the buried money. Perhaps he feared that his rescuers would claim a share in salvage. Perhaps he and his crew intended to come back and to reclaim the money for themselves.

Rattenbury returned to Lord Howe in 1831. Tradition has it that he had buried the money at the foot of Mount Gower. He now discovered that there had been a considerable landslide. The cache was buried beneath tons of rocks and soil. The landscape was so altered that he could not recognize the precise spot. Subsequent enquiries have confirmed the essential facts of this story, but the sovereigns—unless Rattenbury returned one day on his own—have never been found.

King Lobengula's Ox-Wagons

King Lobengula of the Matabele tribe led his warriors against Mashonaland in 1893. Troops of the British South Africa Company eventually defeated him on 1 November of that year at Bembesi river, north-east of his capital, Bulawayo. His palace was captured, but he managed to escape, it is said, with ten ox-wagons laden with gold, ivory and unpolished diamonds.

He and a small group of warriors deposited this treasure in a cavity hollowed out in the rock at a lonely valley said to have been 'at several days march' from the last battle. On their return to the main body, Lobengula ordered the execution of his assistants. Only his secretary, John Jacobs, survived. It is to him that we owe the treasure story. Lobengula died in 1894. In 1943, his grave was discovered in Southern Rhodesia. Many expeditions have been made in search of the Matabele treasure. Some have included John Jacobs. None has succeeded.

This story possesses many of the dubious characteristics to which treasure-hunters soon become accustomed: the solitary questionable source; the implausible size of the hoard; the imprecision of the directions. There are many reasons for which Jacobs may have found a treasure story convenient. He may have deserted Lobengula and sought to vindicate himself; he

mention of the money when they were rescued soon after, and in 1831 Rattenbury returned to the island but was prevented from reclaiming it by a recent landslide.

may have protected himself on capture by the importance which a sole guide to an enormous treasure inevitably acquires.

Yet the story illustrates something positive too. It is unlikely, whatever Jacobs's motives for exaggerating the size of the hoard, that he would have thought he would be believed unless Lobengula could reasonably be thought to have had gold and diamonds as his portable tribal wealth. On the 'no smoke without fire' principle, I feel inclined to believe that the mineral-rich Matabele must have had some such hoard, that Lobengula would have had control of it and that there was no sign of it a year later when Lobengula died. Jacobs may have received his information at second or third hand, but there was some such information to be had. Start modestly from this premise, question Jacobs's authority and we end up with a treasure somewhat smaller but no less interesting.

Modern Treasure

There are great modern treasures still awaiting discovery, most of them lost as a consequence of social upheaval. There must be many Imperial treasures still lying where they were hastily buried in the chaos and panic of the Bolshevik Revolution in Russia, many religious treasures hidden in the mountains of Tibet. The Second World War, of course, displaced millions of people and saw valuables looted, stolen and hidden all over Europe. The greatest of the Second World War treasures, however, possibly excluding a great hoard of looted paintings now reputed to be stored in Tangiers, is thought to be *bona fide* Nazi wealth concealed somewhere on a Mediterranean island.

Rommel's Gold, Silver and Diamonds

Field Marshal Erwin Rommel had instructions from his *führer* which sound like a game of *Risk*. He was to break through Egypt, annexe the Middle East, march through India and join up with the Germans' Japanese allies.

Rommel was a fine general and a practical man. He refused to accept deutschmarks as Hitler at first suggested. He wanted to know that he could buy fuel for his army at any point in the journey without delay and insisted that he be equipped therefore with gold, silver and diamonds.

After his defeat at El Alamein, Rommel withdrew from Egypt to Tunisia, from Tunisia to Sicily, with the Allied troops hot on his heels. As the Third Reich tottered, Hitler ordered his greatest general to the Western front.

Italy had just surrendered. Rommel could not leave his treasure in Sicily or Sardinia. He therefore ordered that it should be taken in a submarine to Corsica, which was still in Axis hands and hidden there until it could be retrieved by the government. In April 1943, German naval officers are said to have concealed a fortune in precious minerals and diamonds somewhere in the *maquis*, the mountains or the bays. They landed on the east coast by night. That is all we know.

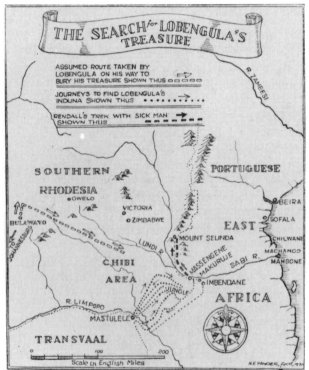

Map showing some of the many expeditions to find Lobengula's wealth. Lloyd Ellis, one of the keenest searchers, spent many years trying to find an 'induna', or minor chieftain, of Lobengula's, who had survived and knew the secret. When at last he came face to face with him, the old man fixed him with a meaningless smile: his mind had gone, and Ellis's search had been in vain.

The sailors reboarded, but an American B44 was on their trail. The U-boat was lost with all hands and Rommel himself, of course, was killed within months.

This story provokes by reason of its plausibility. It has been widely recounted ever since the war and is firmly believed by the Corsicans themselves. If ever a truly giant treasure is to be found on land, it will spring from circumstances like these. The sinking of the submarine is an accredited fact. Rommel must have had substantial army funds and is known to have disliked relying on paper money with which to buy goodwill and assistance on his campaigns. Many searches have been made, but, if the treasure is there, it could remain undiscovered for centuries, so wide is the area of search. In 1961, a diver established a diving-school in the Gulf of Valinco on the south-eastern tip of the island. 'There were no pupils, but there was a lot of diving done,' said John Lucarotti, a writer who lives in Ajaccio, 'Everyone was curious.' One day, the diver was found harpooned with his own spear-gun. This is one of several such instances of violent death amongst treasure-seekers. The natives believe that someone still guards Rommel's treasure.

Criminal Treasure

The third major reason for hiding wealth is crime and fear of discovery. Here the hunter should primarily beware of the philosopher's stone of romance. Piracy, whether in a 'political' or in a personal cause, is no more glamorous than the waffling and squabbling of a pack of jackals over the corpse of a lion. Occasionally pirates would find a great prize. More frequently, after considerable bloodshed, they would net little more than a few arms, a few women for their use, a few prisoners to be sold as slaves, a little money, jewellery and other personal effects which would quickly be squandered. Pirates lived dangerous lives and spent money 'like there was no tomorrow'. A few intelligent corsairs and pirate chiefs may have hoarded their wealth with a view to respectable retirement, but most pirate gold ended up not in chests on desert islands but in the whorehouses of Port Royal or Tahiti, or at the bottom of the sea.

Contrary to popular legend, too, governments and merchant seamen were not generally foolish. Knowing of pirates' existence, they sent their bullion ships to sea well-manned and bristling with arms. Effective piracy therefore, like terrorism today, was a capital-intensive business. Pirate sloops needed to be quick, modern, extremely well-armed and equipped, and fully crewed. Few cargoes exceed the value of the ships that bear them. At a conservative estimate, therefore, at least half of an efficient pirate's earnings must be reinvested. The crew must then be given its share to squander. Relating possible earnings to costs and to risks, piracy is a very bad business prospect indeed.

The Story of Captain Kidd

A classic illustration of the manner in which popular history enhances the reputation of a pirate and of his treasure is the story of Captain Kidd.

William Kidd was a British naval officer who had distinguished himself in action against the French in the Caribbean. In 1695, he received William III's commission to capture pirates and to confiscate their booty. He himself turned pirate. It seems that he hoped merely to make a quick fortune and to remain unrecognized. He was shocked and dismayed to find himself outlawed.

The richest prize that Kidd captured was the *Quedagh Merchant*, which was carrying some £60,000 worth of varied cargo. £10,000 worth was sold off—presumably at a criminal discount—and distributed to the crew. Kidd left the *Quedagh Merchant* at Anguilla on learning that it was being sought. He sold more of the cargo at Hispaniola in order to buy a new sloop, the *San Antonio*. He left some more of the booty with John Gardiner on Long Island, then reported to John Bellamont, Governor of New England, in order to protest his innocence. Bellamont promptly clapped him in irons, seized £14,000 worth of goods and the *San Antonio*, and dispatched Kidd back to be executed at Wapping Old Stairs on 23 May 1701.

On the eve of his execution, Kidd made a last bid to postpone the evil day. He wrote to Robert Harley, the speaker of the House of Commons. 'I have lodged goods and treasure to the value of

The romanticized view of pirates and buried treasure,
encouraged by such images as this, all too often conceals
the fact that most pirates were bloodthirsty thieves and murderers.

£100,000 in the Indies.' Harley rightly disregarded this absurd claim, but treasure hunters, who often think that they know better than the man on the spot, have not shown such intelligent scepticism. Millions of pounds have been spent and many lives risked in pursuit of the doubtful 'Treasure of Captain Kidd'.

Pirate Treasure

This is not to say that there are not buried pirate treasures. Many pirates had their governments' approval and financial backing in their bid to control the trade routes. They could therefore make substantial profits without excessive outlay and might frequently choose to bury some part of their plunder rather than sharing it with their backers.

Some sage individual pirates too, may have deposited their small shares of booty in deserted spots. They had no banks, after all, and no means to remit money to their families. Whilst they kept their wealth about them, it was constantly at risk from other crew members. These small caches are more frequently found than the great prizes of legend.

What we must look for, therefore, is not the romantic figures, the famous villains, who have been glorified in penny dreadfuls, melodramas and films—their names are naturally associated with treasure (frequently they acquired their fame by false claims of hidden wealth)—but the particular circumstances which might cause a pirate chief to hide his booty.

In general, I believe that the best candidates are pirates who are already rich or well subsidized and can thus afford to 'bank' their liquid funds, or those in immediate danger of capture and so with good reason to retain their treasure. This last seems, I know, an odd concept. It would appear evident that any thief would wish to retain wealth, but great pirate chiefs knew that they had an appointment with the hangman when once they were caught. There would be little reason to part with treasure in the course of an unpredictable and nomadic life unless the pirate had cause to suppose that he or his descendants were likely to be able to retrieve it. Few pirate chiefs had legitimate descendants.

The great hoards are more likely, too, to come from single, well-documented crimes. If a pirate hoards his accumulated wealth aboard his ship, he is likely to continue to hoard his accumulated wealth aboard his ship. If he is, as it were, an irregular pirate—an opportunist who has committed a crime and wishes to return to respectable life, or who has cause to fear detection in consequence of his possession of the plunder —then he is likely to hide it away.

Pirates were literally terrorists. Terror was the most powerful weapon in their armoury. They would not have objected therefore to the vastly exaggerated tales of their evil doings which were told by a sensation-hungry public. They may

indeed have fostered them. Edward Teach, otherwise known as Blackbeard, wove smoking fuses into his hair and beard. Lolonois is said to have torn the heart out of one of his victims and eaten it *pour encourager les autres*. The tales of savagery and of wealth proliferate and grow less and less plausible as they pass into folklore. Again, this does not mean that they do not contain some small grain of truth which may lead to treasure.

Mugnoz, Wanda and the Aruba Hoard

The story of Domingo Mugnoz is a delightful example of the *genre*. It has truth at its core. It even has a large amount of psychological verisimilitude.

Mugnoz was the parish priest of Sagraro in the city of Quito, Columbia in 1819 or thereabouts. Amongst his parishioners was a blonde Russian woman named Wanda (according to another source, a Spaniard named Rosita). She lived in a hacienda, just outside Quito, unhappily married to one Pedro de Cires whom she had met in the United States.

Wanda had a French lover named Maurel. Her husband knew of the liaison and tolerated it. Mugnoz felt compelled to set this scandalous state of affairs to rights. One night he drove Maurel out of his own house and returned the half-naked Wanda to her husband. Soon afterwards, rebels obliged the Spanish to quit Quito. De Cires fled with Wanda, a lame black servant named Congo and Fr. Mugnoz. He rented a house on the River Guayra in Caracas and started to trade with the Indians. Mugnoz had by now become Wanda's lover.

One night, de Cires was found stabbed to death. Mugnoz and Congo were gaoled awaiting trial for murder. They were freed by a general amnesty declared when Bolivar's troops, under General Paez, took Caracas.

Mugnoz left prison with Congo and a band of followers. It seems that the priest's principles had been gradually eroded. There is something more than plausible in the process which we observe here. A conscientious, guilt-ridden man, already damned thanks to Wanda's seductive powers, now resolves to damn himself thoroughly. He retrieved Wanda and vanished with his rabble.

This eighteenth-century scene of a pirate being hanged beside the River Thames is a reminder of the grim reality of a sea-robber's life. The story of Captain Kidd is a notable example.

A horrifying story of piracy appeared in the Jamaican newspapers on 4 August 1822, nearly two years after Mugnoz was released from gaol. The *Blessing*, a sloop returning from Cuba to Orabessa, had been captured by a large schooner named the *Emmanuel* which sailed under a black flag. When Captain Smith of the *Blessing* proved unable to offer any ransom save his cargo, he was forced to walk the plank. He was shot as he tried to swim back to the ship. His fourteen year old son was distressed and 'tired of his screams and sobs, the savage captain let fly a blow to his head with the butt end of his musket, seized him by his feet and threw him into the sea'.

This pirate captain then fired the ship and forced his prisoners into a longboat with a jar of water and a day's ration of sea biscuit. He could have no reason to suppose that they would survive, but a schooner picked them up that same afternoon and put in at Port Morant on 18 July. The first mate filed a report on this event to Admiral Ferguson, the senior naval officer, and left a brief description of the pirate captain. At the time his name was unknown. Soon the whole seaboard was to know it: Mugnoz.

In the next three years, Mugnoz terrorized the Southern Caribbean, plundering trading-ships, sometimes massacring their crews. These orgies of violence again seem compatible with the concept of the sensuous man racked by moral guilt.

All the plunder was taken to one of two bases which Mugnoz had established—one in the heights of Northern Cuba and another on the island of Aruba, a few miles off Cape San Roman on the north coast of Venezuela.

Aruba is 17 miles long and has a steep mountain known as *Cerrito Colorado*, the Red Hill, at its southern tip. The only anchorage is provided by a bay close by which is attained through a narrow and dangerous channel. Here, high on the mountain's slopes, in a cavern or network of caverns, Mugnoz established his citadel.

Again and again the stories came in of the ritual burning of prisoners by Mugnoz and a black man with a limp. Again and again, too, we hear of Wanda, who was clearly unbalanced or mentally retarded and, it would seem, of uninhibited sexuality. She is never recorded as wearing more than a short dress and often went naked, wearing only plundered rings and bracelets. One of Mugnoz' followers, a Spaniard called Diaz, who was captured off Porto Rico by the *New York*, told of quasi-religious rituals performed by Mugnoz in his three 'chapels', one on board the *Emmanuel* and one at each of his bases. At these masses, Congo seems to have been chief torturer and Wanda one, at least, of the objects of devotion. At the climax of the ceremony, Mugnoz would hand her over to his crew.

In 1825, Mugnoz's gang was disbanded. The plunder was shared out and Mugnoz and Wanda retired to Aruba. Congo was captured and confessed, corroborating Diaz's evidence and adding the information that the treasure was buried on the Cerrito Colorado. Admiral Padilla of the coastal police descended on Aruba and sent thirty men to search the mountain. They found the remains of ships' sails, a long chain attached to a stake with a manacle at its further end and a number of tools. They also found an underground chapel with an altar still bedecked with flowers and strewn with various religious paraphernalia.

Thus runs the story of the Aruba treasure. A fine, colourful story it is too, but our problem is that more and more colour has been added with each retelling. It is possible—even likely—that a renegade priest, besotted with a deranged woman, turned pirate, indulged in sacrilegious orgies and at last vanished. It is even possible that he amassed a considerable hoard of plunder, but our only source as to the whereabouts of the treasure is the doubtful Congo. For all the embroidery of the story, I would still deem it worthwhile to disembark with a metal detector if I were passing Aruba.

The Lesson of El Dorado

There is one sort of treasure which does not owe its existence to human anguish or death, that is, the votive offering or sacrifice which gave rise to the legend of El Dorado.

In 1519, the *conquistadores* under Cortes swept into Mexico. They found large quantities of gold religious artefacts and jewellery in the cities of the Mayans and the Aztecs. They saw pieces of gold jewellery worn even by the common people. They were astonished to see gold objects thrown into deep lakes never to be retrieved, and they jumped to all the wrong conclusions. They assumed that there were great mines being worked in the interior and they tortured many Indians to find out where they were. They wrote home to tell of mountains of gold, wells of gold, cities built of gold, and more settlers came, lured by these tales. Long after the Spaniards had been driven from the Americas, the legend endured. Many hundreds of treasure hunters have wasted their lives—and frequently lost them—in the quest for this great source of wealth.

The Mexican Indians were largely neolithic—their swords, for example, were of obsidian, not of metal. The gold and silver objects which so excited the Spaniards had been accumulated over many centuries. They had not been mined, but beaten or worked from nuggets found in streams or from ore found on or close to ground level. There was, of course, enormous mineral wealth to be mined in Mexico, as the Jesuits were soon to prove, but the Indians had not mined it. The Spanish soldiers, however, reasoned that, if the gold had not been mined, it must have come from some extraordinary central source. Brutish and greedy, they plundered the Aztec empire and moved on into Peru, killing and raping, looting and torturing, and all for nothing. If they had bothered to roll up their sleeves and start digging, they would have ended up infinitely richer, and great civilizations would have been saved.

The relatively cavalier attitude of the Indians to their gold derived not from profligate wealth but from a social and economic structure different from any that the Spanish had ever seen. The economy was founded upon barter. Gold was sacred or decorative. Sacred or decorative things are, of their nature, to a large extent shared.

As to the custom of throwing precious goods into the river, this is found throughout Central and South American Indian cultures. Most of the ancient Indian towns were built beside deep lakes. These life-giving lakes had their own gods who must be propitiated and appeased if the waters were not to dry up. Many young men and women were sacrificed to the lake gods, and many valuable articles were also thrown into the lake in the course of their ceremonies.

Again, this was misunderstood, and when the Spaniards heard the tale of *El Dorado* (i.e. the gilded man) he was rapidly converted into the golden man; King, of course, of a country of gold.

The origin of this tale is to be found in the

Lake Guatavita, high in the Andes, was formerly a sacred site for the Chibcha tribe of Colombia. They would celebrate the crowning of their new king by covering him in gold dust from head to toe and sending him out into the centre of the lake on a raft. From there he and four companions would throw precious offerings into the water. Out of confused accounts of this ceremony grew the legend of El Dorado, the golden man.

Amongst the votive offerings of the Chibcha was this
beautiful representation of the new king and his attendants
on their raft.

coronation ceremony of the Chibcha in
Colombia. The people worshipped the god of
Lake Guatavita, one of five sacred lakes high in
the eastern *cordillera* of the Andes. The new king
was stripped naked, covered in 'a sticky earth' and
then sprinkled with gold dust so that he was
literally gilded from head to toe. He then stood
stock still upon a raft as his subjects piled gold and
treasure around his feet. His four principal
subjects joined him on the raft and together they
floated out to the centre of the lake, where the
monarch and his ministers threw all the offerings
into the water.

The legend was told and retold and became
more and more exaggerated. The Spanish
actually came to Lake Guatavita in 1539 but
found no golden buildings or streets and passed
on. They claimed all the territory between the
Andes and the Orinoco and named it the Province
of El Dorado.

Many great expeditions were sent in search of
this magical land. Quesada spent four years and
lost 934 soldiers in the quest between 1568 and
1572. Berrio made three expeditionary journeys
between 1584 and 1591 before being captured by
Sir Walter Ralegh, who sacrificed a brilliant
career, all his money and finally his life in pursuit
of the legendary kingdom.

In 1578 a wine merchant named Antonio
Sepulveda lowered the water level in Lake
Guatavita by having a huge notch cut in the rim of
the lake. In the twenty metres or so of mud which
was thus exposed, he picked up hundreds of
wrought gold figures, a staff covered with gold
plates and ornaments, and an emerald 'the size
of a hen's egg'. It is said that he employed 8,000
men to do the work. Once the government had
received its share of the find, Sepulveda was
bankrupt.

Many have followed in his footsteps. In 1898, a
Company for the Exploitation of the Lagoon of
Guatavita attempted to drain the lake but failed.
Later, between 1905 and 1909, Contractors Ltd.,
a British firm, succeeded in draining the lake, but

the thick mud at the centre had been baked hard before they could search it. They too went bankrupt, though they had found much gold.

In 1965, the Colombian government at last showed some sensibility and declared the lake to be a protected area of natural and cultural interest. There will be no more drainages.

The legend of El Dorado illustrates just about every fault of which the treasure hunter must beware: exaggeration, the tendency to set one's sights on what one would like to find rather than what is likely to be found, obsessiveness, over-investment, greed, romancing and downright ignorance. As the other stories have shown, treasure hunting can never hope to be an exact science. Nonetheless, in treasure hunting we have the chance to make use of as much common sense and learning as we possess. The detailed accounts of great lost treasures in the main part of this book give us the chance to do so.

AGRIHAN, MARIANA ISLANDS, NORTH PACIFIC
SOUTH AMERICAN PIRATE BOOTY

This tale of cruelty, theft and bloodshed, starts incongruously amidst the sacred music, fragrant incense smoke and airy light of a Lima church in 1826. Among the congregation that morning were a Scottish adventurer with the unusual name of Roberton and a young beauty named Teresa Mendez. Roberton watched her with interest and at the end of the service enquired about her. He learned that she was only twenty-one and the wealthy widow of a Spanish sea-captain. Inevitably, she had many suitors. She encouraged them, although insisting only on those of rank, wealth or noble birth.

Roberton was stricken and set about wooing her. When he declared his love, she laughed. It was obvious to all but him that he had none of the qualities that she demanded. It was probably only to amuse her friends that she promised herself to him if only he could find the means to support her in the style to which she wished to become accustomed.

Roberton racked his brains. He was still racking them when he attended a gathering of naval officers at Callao. Gabriel Lafond de Lurcy, author of *Voyages Autour du Monde* and our primary source for this story, was present. Roberton's predicament was well known, and a Lieutenant Vieyra laughingly remarked that he would have no further problems if only he could take over the *Peruano*, an English vessel then lying in harbour. The *Peruano* had been the subject of such remarks ever since she berthed. She was known to be carrying war funds totalling 2,000,000 gold piastres.

Roberton, according to Lafond, smiled politely and did not pursue the subject, but that night in the harbour he rounded up a gang of brigands, mostly British sailors from his own frigate, and attacked the poorly defended vessel. By dawn, he was far away and heading south west before a strong prevailing breeze. The members of the crew on shore-leave found their ship gone and raised the alarm, but Roberton's start was too great.

At first sight, Roberton's impulsive and implausible action seems like many another travellers' tale of the sort which abounded in the turbulent years when the emerging Americas fought to expel their Spanish overlords. We have grown rightly sceptical of many of these stories, for folklore makes romantic outlaws of squalid, small-time extortionists, or great pirate chiefs of brutish, self-seeking terrorists. Roberton's existence, however, is beyond doubt, as is the fact that he was a professional sailor and ruthless adventurer. We are fortunate to know enough of his career and his character to recognize that spontaneous piracy was entirely consistent with his record.

Roberton—Mercenary and Pirate

In the same war which saw another Scotsman, William Thompson, sailing to Cocos Island with a great treasure of Lima, Roberton was to be found fighting for the Chileans in their ultimately successful bid to rid themselves of Spanish domination. A Glaswegian from a naval family, Roberton had been a low-ranking British naval officer. In 1817, he became First Lieutenant aboard the Chilean man-of-war, *Galvarino*, first under Captain Guise, then one Captain Stary.

In 1820, Lieutenant Gabriel Lafond was sailing from San-Blas to Guayaquil as second-in-

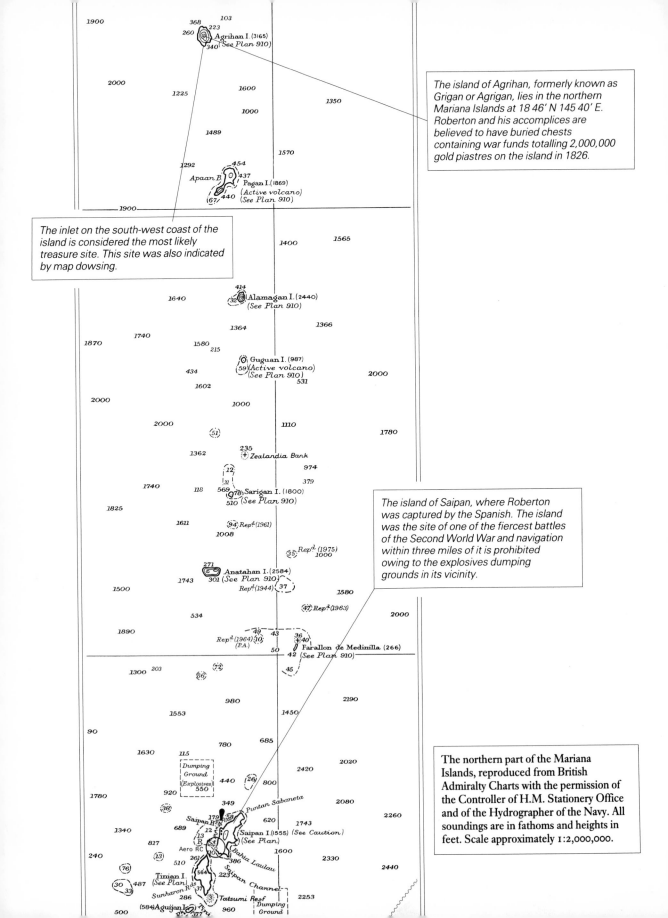

The island of Agrihan, formerly known as
Grigan or Agrigan, lies in the northern
Mariana Islands at 18 46' N 145 40' E.
Roberton and his accomplices are
believed to have buried chests
containing war funds totalling 2,000,000
gold piastres on the island in 1826.

The inlet on the south-west coast of the
island is considered the most likely
treasure site. This site was also indicated
by map dowsing.

The island of Saipan, where Roberton
was captured by the Spanish. The island
was the site of one of the fiercest battles
of the Second World War and navigation
within three miles of it is prohibited
owing to the explosives dumping
grounds in its vicinity.

The northern part of the Mariana
Islands, reproduced from British
Admiralty Charts with the permission of
the Controller of H.M. Stationery Office
and of the Hydrographer of the Navy. All
soundings are in fathoms and heights in
feet. Scale approximately 1:2,000,000.

command of an American trading vessel, *Mentor*. The vessel was neutral, but her Commander, Captain Gardiner, was under no illusions as to the ethics of the rebellious Chileans. Lafond was instructed to remain alert.

The *Mentor*, however, was heavily laden and cumbersome. The *Galvarino* was fast, armed and easily manoeuvrable. Roberton came on board to find out who and what was aboard the *Mentor* and to consider what action should be taken. The two seconds-in-command, Roberton and Lafond, the Scotsman and the Frenchman, thousands of miles from their own nations, confronted one another across the deck.

Lafond records his first impression of Roberton as an ill-favoured man of medium build with reddish brown hair, a flushed complexion and cruel, clear blue eyes. He gave terse and authoritative orders. Whilst the captain was a more prepossessing man, Lafond was in no doubt that Roberton was really in charge and wrote later:

Robertson (sic) était brave jusqu'à l'excès, son caractère fougueux et passioné le rendait souvent farouche et cruel. Il avait la taille moyenne, les cheveux rouges, le regard fauve, et quoique ses traits n'eussent pas précisément de la laideur, son aspect était repoussant.

[Robertson (*sic*) was exceedingly bold, his impetuous and fiery character making him often savage and cruel. He was of medium height, with red hair, a wild look, and while he wasn't exactly ugly, he was a repugnant sight.]

He also added that Roberton had the grin of a hyena.

Without regard to international laws, Roberton was all for compelling an officer and half the crew of the *Mentor* to disembark into the *Galvarino*, but fog and the approach of an American warship interceded to prevent him, and he left empty-handed.

Gabriel Lafond, seen here interviewing blacks in Manila, was an adventurous young Frenchman whose interesting travels included several meetings with the Scottish pirate, Roberton. Fascinated by this man, he researched the facts of Roberton's extraordinary life and described them in his *Voyages autour du Monde*, published after his return to France in about 1840.

Two years later, he is found chasing a bandit named Benavides, who fled inland from the Chilean coastal town of Arauco. There he captured a friend of Benavides, named Pacheco, and extracted information from him by whipping. Soon afterwards, he took Benavides and his men by surprise and captured all except for Benavides himself and his lieutenant, an Italian called Martelin.

Roberton hanged all of them—some sixty or seventy men, in a clearing. Legend, which may reflect the truth or may merely reflect the awe in which this man was held, has it that suddenly taken with the idea of a complete circle of hanging bodies, he completed it with the corpses of some Spaniards who had been killed in the original attack.

Interlude on Mocha

Soon after this, Roberton resigned from the navy and went to live on a small, fertile, deserted island called Mocha, seventy-five miles south of the bay of Concepcion, Chile. He seems to have started a small settlement. Aside from two devoted women and a black servant, he brought several other colonists—perhaps fellow ex-naval men—with him. Here we must rely on hearsay as to his real intentions. There is a story that Benavides had buried his loot on Mocha and that Roberton had extracted indications as to the cache's whereabouts by torture from one of the brigands whom he hanged. However that may be, most of Roberton's companions—one of them his brother—were drowned when a whale-boat foundered on the way back from Valdivia, and Roberton soon left Mocha and volunteered for the Peruvian navy. We hear of him capturing the French *Vigie* off Arica and narrowly escaping from the *Quintanilla*, a Spanish frigate under the command of Benavides's former lieutenant, Martelin. He distinguishes himself at the siege of Lima, is imprisoned, escapes and is reinstated in the navy.

And then, a man known for ruthlessness, a successful, daring and strangely solitary man, meets Teresa Mendez and her unthinking taunt provokes him to an act of piracy, for once, on his own account.

The Treasure of the *Peruano*

The *Peruano* sailed for Tahiti. Immediate pursuers had been left far behind, but Roberton knew well that within days he would be the quarry of a serious and organized hunt. He urged his rabble of a crew to abandon their merrymaking on Tahiti and to sail for some more deserted spot. They were reluctant, but Roberton's trusted henchmen, Irishmen whom we know only as George and William, rounded them up and, by a combination of violent threats and the inducement of fifteen Tahitian girls whom they had brought on board, persuaded them once more to set sail.

Roberton needed men to help him to get away, but he seems to have had no intention of sharing his treasure with anyone save Teresa. At one desert island where he put in for water, he marooned eight of his men, claiming that they had been plotting against him. He then headed northwest for the Mariana archipelago, and after investigating various islands in the group anchored in a bay of one known on the French charts as Grigan or Agrigan, and now known as Agrihan.

The first task to be carried out was the wholesale slaughter of the women, largely carried out by William who was an expert marksman. Although several swam for the shore and some attained it, none survived. The seven remaining men now carried the chests of gold coins ashore and buried them at a short distance from the sea in a clearing that they had prepared at the foot of a cliff. They chopped down and marked a few trees on the site and left marks on rocks and trees between the shoreline and the clearing to guide them on their return.

They re-embarked and Roberton prepared for the final stage of his plan, in which George and William were willing, not to say eager assistants. Approaching the mainland, they would scuttle the ship with the remaining crew trapped within her, below hatches. Close to the Hawaiian Islands, they sealed the hatches and removed the cocks, then rowed ashore in a lifeboat. They landed at Oahu, one of the islands, claiming to have been shipwrecked. They had reserved 20,000 piastres from the treasure for their own use.

What they did not realize as they celebrated their success and enjoyed the traditional Hawaiian Islands welcome was that they had failed to scuttle the ship properly. It drifted about for some weeks, low in the water but still afloat, until a passing whaler saw it and investigated. They found three men who had starved to death and a fourth barely clinging to life. They took him aboard, but it was a full year before he reached land—also at Oahu. He was to recount his story to Lafond in 1828.

George soon disappeared in Rio de Janeiro, presumably killed by his fellow conspirators. Now Roberton and William were never apart, each terrified that the other might steal a march on the other or stab him in the back. In 1827, they were in Hobart, Tasmania, where they persuaded an old sailor named Thomson to take his schooner on the long journey back to Agrihan. They set out with a small crew, and the inquisitive Thomson managed to coax from William, while drunk, the true purpose of the voyage. William did not know the name of the island where they had left the treasure. He identified it only as an island north of Saipan and Tinian, two other islands in the Marianas group.

William was the next to go. Thomson awoke one night with a start to hear his last scream. There could be little doubt as to the identity of the murderer. Thomson was now doubly vigilant, but Roberton was not to be thwarted and the old man was pushed overboard.

Thomson refused to die. He was picked up, more dead than alive, by a Spanish ship which swiftly pursued Roberton to Saipan where, abandoning the vessel and retreating inshore, he was captured and clapped in irons. Thomson, who had sailed these seas, was certain from William's description that the treasure island must be Agrihan. The Spaniards took Roberton to the island. He revealed nothing. He wandered about in a somewhat aimless way, tried to escape his captors and was dragged back to the ship. There, he was flogged over a cannon until he gave his word that he would guide them properly. Roberton had just one more card to play. He could not win, but he did not intend that anyone else should either. As they rowed him ashore in the dinghy, he threw himself over the side and was dragged by his chains to the bottom.

A view of Saipan, showing terrain typical of the Mariana islands. Here, in 1827, the Spanish intercepted Roberton on his way back to Agrihan to reclaim his treasure.

The Secret of Agrihan

After his death, Medinilla, the Spanish governor of the Marianas, employed six hundred natives to search for the chests. They excavated tons of sand and earth but came away empty-handed. It may seem incredible that so large a force failed to discover the treasure on a small Pacific island, but when we consider the practical problems involved in searching a fertile, uninhabited island, the continued existence of the treasure seems more likely. Agrihan measures 6 miles long by 3½ miles wide and is surrounded by limestone cliffs. If, as Lafond reports, Roberton buried the stolen gold somewhere up an inlet, and took pains to cover his tracks, then a mass treasure-hunting expedition armed only with spades and pickaxes probably did come away empty-handed.

FURTHER ACTION

Agrihan lies at 18° 46′ N 145° 40′ E, and contains the highest peak of the Marianas group at 3,166 ft. The nearest island with regular air service is Guam, the southernmost island in the group, and an American base since the end of the Second World War.

The inlet on the south-west coast is the most likely site. Nonetheless, a thorough search of any inlets on the island with non-discriminating, all-metal detectors with a depth potential of several feet would be essential. The size of the hoard, the likely absence of interference from other objects and the possibility of limiting the search zones are all in the favour of this approach. The Marianas are US territory and US treasure trove laws apply.

Voyages Autour du Monde by Gabriel Lafond (de Lurcy) is the original source of this treasure story. Further knowledge about Medinilla's (the Spanish governor of the Marianas in 1827/8) search for the treasure, would be reassuring, as would any further details of the Spanish ship which captured Thomson on Saipan and took him to Agrihan.

The southernmost island of the Mariana group, Guam has been an American base since the end of the war. It is the nearest point to Agrihan with a regular air service.

BASING HOUSE, BASINGSTOKE, HAMPSHIRE, ENGLAND
CATHOLIC TREASURE FROM THE CIVIL WAR

The possibility of the existence of a great treasure beneath the ruins of Basing House in Hampshire is based upon local legend and family tradition, but at several points legend, history and archaeology meet in a manner which suggests that the full story of the siege and destruction of this great secular palace remains to be uncovered.

Nonetheless, the story as it stands is remarkable in itself, for it is the dreadful tale of the collapse of one of the final Royalist strongholds in the English Civil war and of a beleaguered garrison who endured the longest siege in English history.

The Siege of Basing House

Basing Castle, the Seat and Mansion of the Marquisse of Winchester, stands on a rising ground, having its forme circular, encompassed with a Brick Rampart, lyned with earth and a very deep trench, but dry. The loftie Gate-house with foure Turrets looking Northwards, on the right whereof without the compasse of the Ditch a goodly building containing two faire Courts ... the place seated and built as if for Royaltie having a proper Motto, Aymez Loyalte [Love Loyalty]. Hither (the Rebellion having made houses of pleasure more unsafe) the Marquisse first retired, hoping integrity and privacy might have here preserved his quiet.

When these words were written around Christmas 1644, the Civil War had entered its third year and any hopes the staunchly Catholic 5th Marquess of Winchester, John Powlett, might once have had of being able to stand aside from the tide of events had long been shattered. Since July 1643 he had kept his house as a garrison for King Charles I and in the intervening period had three times resisted Parliament's attempts to capture it.

From June to November 1644 the house—'the greatest of any subject's house in England, yea, larger than most ... of the King's Palaces'—had been under almost constant siege. In September, when the garrison had been close to surrender, Colonel Henry Gage had come down from the Royalist stronghold at Oxford with 650 men and swept through the besieging army several times the size of his force from the rear. Before the enemy had time to regroup, he delivered his supplies of twelve barrels of powder, food and other provisions, raided Basingstoke for more, and then escaped into the fog.

In October, the King's army of 10,000 men got to within seven miles of the house and then retreated as suddenly as it had come when the Parliamentary forces around Basingstoke swelled to 19,000. On 21 October, the King won the Second Battle of Newbury—one of the few Royalist triumphs of the year—but was unable to return to Basing. In November, the newly knighted Gage returned to find that the besieging army, having dwindled to a mere 700 men, had departed.

But there was to be no happy ending for Basing House. It commanded the road to Salisbury, it was the easternmost of the Royalist garrisons west of London, and it had become a symbol of Royalist and Papist resistance—the Marquess was, indeed, believed to have scratched 'Aymez

This copy of a lost drawing shows the New House at
Basing from the east at the time of the siege.

Loyalte' on every window in the house with his
diamond ring.

During the lull in hostilities Lord Edward
Powlett, the Marquess's brother and a Protestant
convert, had been the most important of a
disaffected group of defenders who had plotted to
surrender the house. Upon discovery, Lord
Edward was pardoned, but forced to act as
executioner to all his fellow conspirators and all
subsequent criminals within the garrison. After
the fall of Basing, the list of prisoners included a
sad entry for 'Edward Pawlet, the hangman'. The
discovery of this plot led to the expulsion of all the
other Protestant soldiers from the house as well as
the able Colonel Royden. They were replaced by
inexperienced Catholic countryfolk described as
'most 18 years old, some not 12'. It was the
beginning of the end.

After a lull of nine months the Roundheads
returned on 20 August under Colonel Dalbier.
Dalbier bombarded Basing continuously. In
September the *Exact Journal* reported: 'Colonel
Dalbere hath raised a battery very near Basing
House. He plays fiercely upon them, hath beat
down one of the towers; he wanted men and more
great guns ... It may be that Lieut.-General
Cromwell may come or send him help.' On 4
October it was reported that, 'Colonel Dalbere
hath made a great breach in Basing House, and
when forces come up as was promised, that he
may block them up round, he will storm ...'

Within the next week Cromwell, who had
recently taken Winchester, sent reinforcements.
He arrived himself with more troops on 11
October and there was now an army of 6,000–
7,000 opposing a force of 300 who included

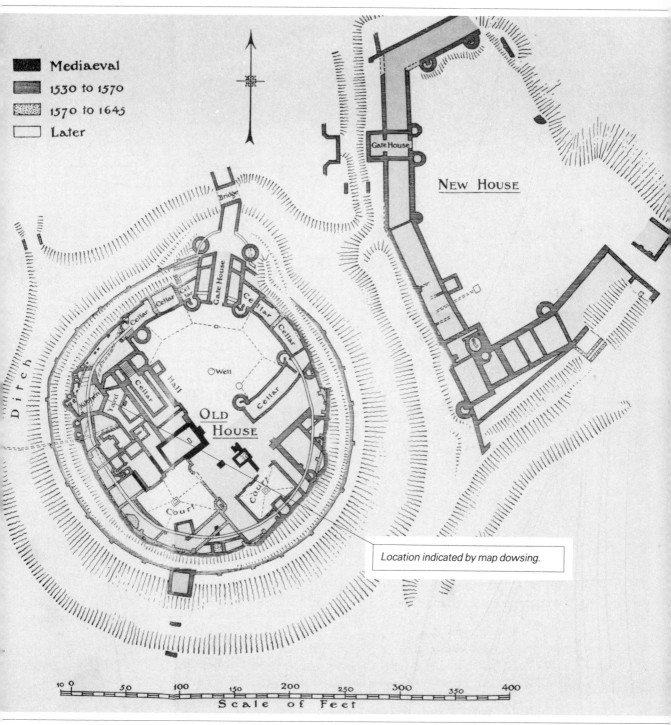

Mediaeval

1530 to 1570

1570 to 1645

Later

Ditch

Bridge

Cellar
Cellar
Cellar
Gate House
Cellar
Cellar
Cellar
Cellar

Well

Hall

Kitchen
Yard

OLD HOUSE

Court
Court
Court

NEW HOUSE

Gate House

Well

Location indicated by map dowsing.

10 0   50   100   150   200   250   300   350   400
S c a l e   o f   F e e t

The only known plan of Basing House made in 1909 by Sir Charles Peers, Secretary of the Society of Antiquities, on the evidence of excavations by William Orde-Powlett, the 4th Baron Bolton at the end of the nineteenth century.

John Powlett, 5th Marquess of Winchester, was the owner of Basing House from the beginning of the Civil War until the end of the siege. Staunchly Royalist and Catholic, he lived to see his king executed and his religion spurned by his own family. He died in 1674 and the poet Dryden honoured him with an epitaph beginning:

He who in impious times undaunted stood,
And midst rebellion durst be just and good,
Whose arms asserted, and whose sufferings more
Confirmed the cause for which he fought before,
Rests here, rewarded by an heavenly prince
For what his earthly could not recompense.

'priests, clergymen, women, sick, wounded, and helpless men'. Not surprisingly, the Royalists who again set out from Oxford to relieve them—the gallant Gage was already dead—thought better of the odds and turned back.

Cromwell summoned the garrison to surrender on the day he arrived. He did not expect they would do so and obviously had no intention of offering a second chance. Not only were they 'a nest of Romanists', but the myth of Basing's resistance needed to be savagely expunged.

The end, when it came, was fast and furious. On the evening of 13 October, the cannons had made two wide breaches, one on the side of the house facing the village, the other on the side facing the park. The final assault came on the following morning:

> Tuesday morning about five of the clocke our forces began to storme the new-house adjoyning to Basing-house, which they tooke after a hot dispute ... They in the old house notwithstanding hung out foure black Ensignes of defiance, and set fire on a bridge over which our men were to passe ... at last our men came on with such courage that they entered the old house too, crying, Fall on, fall on, all is our owne. This was done by seven a clocke that morning.

The sequel was bloody. There were fewer than a hundred prisoners. The Marquess was taken alive, as was Wenceslaus Hollar, the engraver and the famous architect Inigo Jones, who had his clothes stolen and only had a blanket for covering. The looting of the house continued all day. By the time anyone noticed the fire which had started in the roof of the New House, the victors were estimated to have taken booty to the value of £200,000 in contemporary value, including the Marquess's cabinet and jewels worth £50,000. Finally the house, disintegrating in the fire, was literally pulled apart by the soldiers and the surrounding countrymen who had come to watch the spectacle. About a week later it was 'Ordered by the house of Commons that Basing house be demolished, and that all such of the Country as shall assist therein shall have the stones for their pains.' So complete was the destruction that ever since it has been impossible, in the absence of architectural plans, to work out the detailed nature of one of England's greatest palaces.

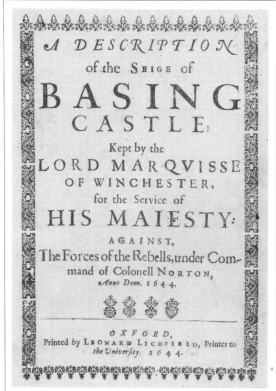

A DESCRIPTION of the SEIGE of BASING CASTLE, Kept by the LORD MARQVISSE OF WINCHESTER, for the Service of HIS MAIESTY: AGAINST, The Forces of the Rebells, under Command of Colonell NORTON, Anno Dom. 1644.

OXFORD, Printed by LEONARD LICHFIELD, Printer to the University. 1644.

The title page of the Royalist pamphlet published just after Parliamentary troops raised their five-month siege in November 1644 and before they returned in August 1645.

The Wealth of the Catholic Families

What has this sad, magnificent story to do with buried treasure? Basing, perhaps the richest house in the kingdom, was sacked, looted and comprehensively demolished. The belief in the existence of undiscovered treasure at Basing, however, comes from the family of the 5th Marquess and bears closer examination.

The story is this. Before the final siege of the house began in August 1645, many of the Catholic families from Hampshire, Berkshire and Wiltshire brought their family treasures to Basing, the premier Catholic fortress in the South. For much of the Civil War they had stood aside from the dispute between King and Parliament, but as Cromwell ran short of funds to pay his troops he began to turn to the Catholics as the easiest means of providing additional revenue.

When the Catholic treasure arrived at Basing it

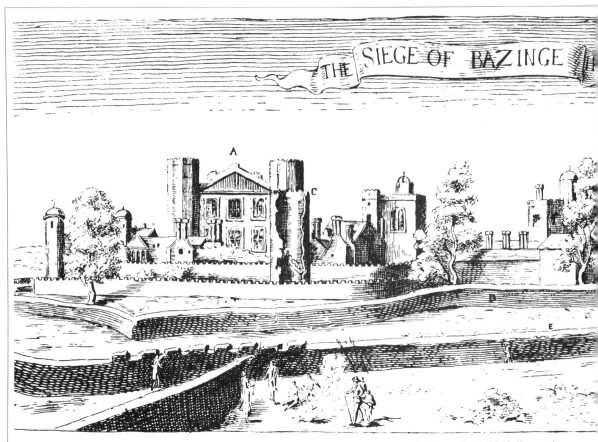

An engraving of Basing House by Wenceslaus Hollar who was amongst those captured at the end of the siege. The Old House is to the left, and the New to the right. In the foreground on the left is 'The Tower that is Halfe Battered Downe'.

was stored in one of the many subterranean rooms or tunnels with which the house abounded and, when the roof collapsed, it was buried forever.

Excavations in the Ruins of Basing House

From as early as 1825 various Lords Bolton, descendants of the 5th Marquess, dug on the site intermittently. Towards the end of the century, the 4th Baron Bolton excavated various parts of the site under the supervision of Sir Charles Peers, and was assisted by an old man in the village named Moss who became a guide to the site. Moss claimed that his great-grandfather had fought in the siege, and provided three legends:

1. The treasure was melted down into a golden calf and two silver calves.
2. The gold was hidden under the 'Jusan' or 'Tusan' tree.
3. There was a 9-foot-tall giant who fought on the side of the defenders in the siege.

Curiously, when the 4th Baron's descendant, Christopher Orde-Powlett renewed his great-grandfather's excavations in the late 1950s, the archaeological group working on the site at his invitation discovered the skeleton of a man measuring 7 ft 3 in by one of the ramparts. All of this seems to tally well with an account contemporary with the siege that 'Amongst those that we saw slaine one of their officers lying on the ground seeming so exceeding tall was measured: and from his great toe to his crown was 9 foot in length measured by a Gentleman of an ordinary size, who was then present.'

Furthermore, the idea that Basing's foundations were, and still are, honeycombed with

some vaults that are farr under ground for their popish priests.' When the house fell six Catholic priests were killed on the spot and four others reserved for a greater, judicial horror. It is not known if any escaped.

In addition to the underground rooms, there were several tunnels, most if not all of which were probably watercourses or drains. The route of one of the tunnels is known today and comes out 80 yards from the Tudor garden opposite the great Tithe Barn. However, two exits from tunnels are known, one half a mile and the other a mile from the house, and it is not clear where, if at all, the entrances are in the house itself.

Although Moss's story of the giant is supported by fact, those of the gold and silver calves and of the 'Jusan tree' are not. The calves sound like the very stuff of myth and seem most likely to have originated in Hugh Peters's sermons about idolatrous worship by the Papist inmates of the house. The 'Jusan tree' on the other hand may be a linguistic corruption of some part of the house. Numerous solutions have been suggested, including '*Jeux Entrée*' (i.e. games entrance) and 'Jews' Sanctuary'. Unfortunately, in the complete absence of details about most parts of the house it is unlikely that this riddle can ever be solved. However, the discovery of 700 gold coins by navvies whilst the Basingstoke canal was being dug through part of the ruins in the 1790s provided more tangible proof of the existence of treasure.

Recent Archaeological Exploration of the Site

Following the excavations of the 4th Baron Bolton, the site was left undisturbed for a number of years until the Hon. Christopher Orde-Powlett began excavations in conjunction with the Aldermaston and Reading archaeological societies in the late 1950s. Despite investigations with an early discriminating metal detector, a mechanical divining machine used for plotting tunnels and a detailed examination of the well, their searches yielded no treasure. However, excavation at the site is a slow, laborious but rewarding business. Basing was continually occupied from Roman times until 14 October 1645 and the remains of the house yield

subterranean passages, tunnels and cellars is substantiated by past and present accounts. The excavations instigated by Christopher Orde-Powlett produced an underground room at the very start and accounts contemporary with the siege yield the following:

> ... there was not above an hundred prisoners in all taken, *besides those who hid themselves in holes*, the rest had no quarter ...

> Mercurius Civicus, 14 Oct., 1645

Riding to the house on Tuesday night, we heard divers crying in vaults for quarter, but our men could neither come to them, nor they to us.

> Hugh Peters

Hugh Peters, who was a Puritan preacher of the Hell Fire school, also recorded that 'there are

In 1965, frogmen from the Royal Engineers descended into the 100-ft.-deep well, but found nothing. The former owner of the site, the Hon. Christopher Orde-Powlett is second from left.

discoveries of great importance to our knowledge of Britain's history and heritage.

FURTHER ACTION

The site has been owned by Hampshire County Council since 1975 and is the subject of a major archaeological dig. For this reason the Basing treasure is emphatically not one for private investigation. This would be not only impractical, but illegal for the ruins are a Grade 2 Ancient Monument and protected by law. Furthermore, in view of the quantity of material of different types the only practical method of search is slow and careful excavation. Happily for anyone interested in being part of the discovery or recovery of Basing's past, Hampshire County Council welcome volunteers to assist them on site in the summer months.

Further documentary evidence, to be found in the notes of the 4th Baron Bolton relating to his excavations, is not at present available. About a week before his death in 1922, he lent them to a bird society, possibly a local one. The notes were not returned, nor have they been since. It must be possible that they survive and they could be very helpful.

BEESTON CASTLE, CHESHIRE, ENGLAND

RICHARD II's WHITE HART TREASURE

The essence of the story is familiar from Shakespeare, how Richard II, the boy king now grown old and persuaded by his countless flatterers of the inviolability of his power, imposed swingeing taxes on his people in the course of his 'second tyranny', seized the estates of his Lancastrian cousins and returned from his campaign in Ireland to find Henry Bolingbroke, the Lancastrian heir, in firm control of his lands.

Beeston Castle, a few miles from Chester and reckoned by many to be the site of a vast fortune left by Richard II in 1398. Searches have concentrated on the well, into which legend claims all the wealth was thrown.

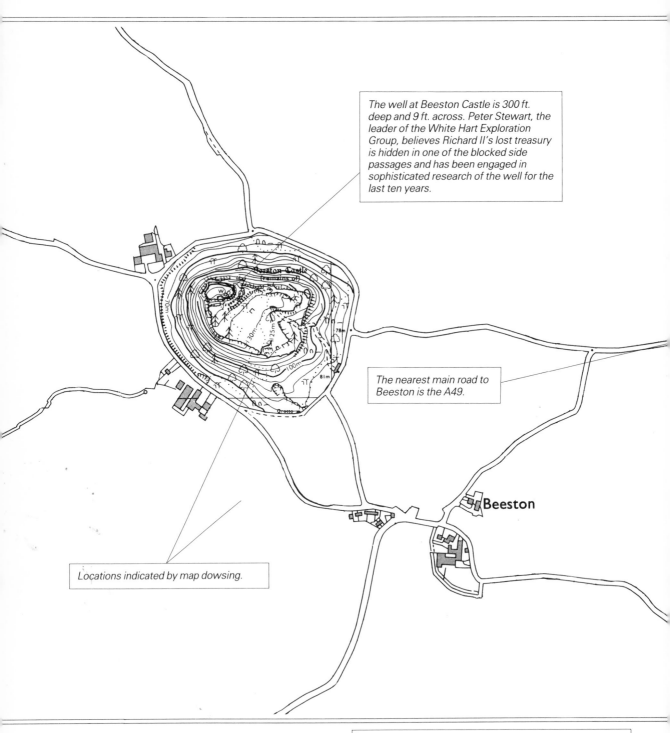

The well at Beeston Castle is 300 ft. deep and 9 ft. across. Peter Stewart, the leader of the White Hart Exploration Group, believes Richard II's lost treasury is hidden in one of the blocked side passages and has been engaged in sophisticated research of the well for the last ten years.

The nearest main road to Beeston is the A49.

Locations indicated by map dowsing.

Beeston

Beeston Castle, Cheshire reproduced from the Ordnance Survey Map (Sheet SJ 55 NW). Crown Copyright reserved. Beeston is situated about ten miles south-west of Chester. Scale 1:10,000.

Richard II remains one of the most elusive and the most fascinating of the medieval kings of England.

Richard was desperate for cash in the months preceding his embarkation for Ireland, and he was reckless as to how it should be raised. He compelled loans from his wealthiest citizens by means of 'letters obligatory' in which they must covenant funds to him by a given date. He concocted 'pardons' for all those who had offended or opposed him, and imposed a burdensome, variable tax named the 'plesaunce' on the seventeen counties that had yet to be pardoned. His appropriation of the vast wealth of 'Harry of Hereford, Lancashire and Derby' on the death of John of Gaunt was a final act of illegal rapacity. He must by now have known that his crown was in danger. It is almost as though now he had ceased to care. His extravagance and vanity were in no way diminished. On his usurpation, the Church commissioners found an enormous store of jewelled clothes which constituted a treasure in themselves. One hardly-worn robe alone was valued at 3,000 marks. A mark was then the equivalent of eight ounces of high assay gold. The coffers, however, were empty. Richard's wealth now consisted in his extraordinary hoard of personal wealth and, like any medieval monarch, who suspects that his power is threatened, he carried his wealth with him.

Jean Creton

Cheshire was the centre of Richard's support. He had even moved his parliament from London to Shrewsbury. In 1398, says Jean Creton, a French knight loyal to Richard in the Earl of Salisbury's retinue, the king deposited 100,000 marks sterling in gold and 100,000 marks in other precious things somewhere in a Cheshire castle plausibly identified as Beeston, a substantial fort set high on a hill near Tarporley, garrisoned by one hundred hand-picked bowmen. This enormous sum represents, according to one contemporary source, just one-sixth of Richard's personal wealth.

We know that Richard took the remainder of his treasury with him to Ireland: '*thesaurum quoque coronas et reliquias aliaque jocalia regni quoque divitias et antiquo dimissas in archivis regni pro honore regni secum abstulit in Hiberniam profecturus sine consensu ... regni sui.*' ('He took with him his treasure, his crowns, his precious objects ... on the point of departing for Ireland without the consent of his kingdom.') This is confirmed by the twenty-third article of his subsequent indictment. On his return from Ireland to find the country up in arms, he left the royal baggage, plate and chapel furniture at Haverfordwest on the Welsh coast. The garrison at Beeston meanwhile surrendered without a struggle to Bolingbroke's troops.

Peter Stewart, an exemplary treasure-seeker, has been working on the Beeston problem for a quarter of a century. 'The unsubstantiated legend,' he says, 'avers that the treasure was thrown down the well in time of war.' This might refer, of course, to some subsequent war, but, since we have no written record that anyone saw the treasure at Beeston after this date, we may be right to assume that the bowmen of Beeston concealed their king's private fund before yielding to the Lancastrians. Stewart is inclined to believe that the well is the likeliest hiding-place, but that the cache is probably in one of a number of side passages which run off the central shaft. The well was cleared in 1842, but the side passages were not explored at that time.

A member of the White Hart Exploration Group descending the well at Beeston Castle. The Group's use of infra-thermal and ultrasonic equipment to search the walls of the well for cavities makes this probably the most sophisticated search of its type ever to have been conducted.

The White Hart Exploration Group

The well at Beeston is 300 ft. deep and 9 ft. across. Some of the side passages were explored in 1935. Stewart first explored them in 1976 as leader of the White Hart Exploration Group, which is named after the personal emblem of Richard of Bordeaux, who distributed White Hart badges to his supporters.

Until the last 100 ft., where it is cut through the solid rock, medieval masonry lines the shaft. Infra-thermal imaging equipment has been unable to detect any cavities behind this masonry. A cesium vapour magnetometer, however, detected various anomalies in 1978. These are still under investigation. Low frequency ultrasonic equipment has also been used to map cavities.

This is probably the most sophisticated search

of its type ever to have been conducted, and Stewart relates that 'the work has already resulted in a complete reappraisal of some standard geophysical techniques and their interpretation'.

In 1984, his team explored a passageway leading off the well 200 ft. down. They found their way blocked by a roof fall. At the time of writing, Stewart plans to use 'some sophisticated equipment for measuring changes in the ground's magnetic field.' If the treasure is indeed in the well, they were brave and resourceful men who hid it.

FURTHER ACTION

Beeston Castle is on the Peckforton Estates. It is under the guardianship of the Department of the Environment from whom permission to dig on the site should be sought. However it is unlikely that a licence would be granted, for the veteran archaeologist Dr C. A. Ralegh Radford is supervising the exhaustive exploration of the site by Peter Stewart. Few people are likely to have a greater chance of finding the treasure than Peter Stewart. He is not only MSc CEng FI Mech E FRAeS MIEE FRPS FBIM, but also Chief of the Advanced Projects Department, Corporate Engineering at Rolls Royce. Nonetheless there could well be a chance of finding more information about the treasure from historical research. Jean Creton's manuscript is in the Harleian Collection of the British Museum. Although it is unlikely that further contemporary accounts will be uncovered local history research may provide additional details of the nineteenth-century clearing of the well and other explorations of the site.

BEN ALDER, NEAR LOCH ERICHT, INVERNESS, SCOTLAND

JACOBITE LOUIS D'OR

The deathblow to the Jacobite cause dealt at the battle of Culloden was rendered doubly shocking for Bonnie Prince Charlie's followers by the cruelty of the English soldiers. The English commander Cumberland justly earned his title 'butcher' when, two days after the battle, a party was detailed to kill all the Scottish wounded still on the battlefield. Amid many acts of inhumanity, and the dogged manhunts for the more illustrious amongst those who managed to escape (including the Prince himself), it is easy to overlook the complex manoeuvrings of certain Jacobites around one final secret that was to bring them endless trouble.

Barrels of *louis d'or* sent to help the Jacobite rebellion were brought to Loch Arkaig from French ships off the coast in May 1746. The gold was buried in two different areas at opposite ends of the loch. In September and October of 1746, Cluny Macpherson transferred the gold to another hiding place.

The Arrival of the French Ships

Less than three weeks after Culloden, at the very beginning of May, 1746, two French ships from Nantes arrived off the west coast of Scotland, in Loch Nan Uamh in Arisaig and anchored in Borrodale. Unaware of the battle, they brought belated supplies for the rebellion, including '1500 Stand of Arms, considerable quantitys of Ammunition, and severall hundred casks of Brandy', but quite the most substantial offering was a total of 35,000 gold *louis*.

The Highlanders fell upon these supplies with gusto, 'beginning with the Brandy, which disappeared in a few hours'. The money alone was spared their attention. It was landed in six casks, which were hurriedly hidden in a wood by certain officers. Two of the Prince's followers, an Irishman and a Lancashireman managed to find the casks and remove one. They took a bag from it containing some 700 *louis d'or*, but later confessed the robbery to a clergyman named Harrison, enabling the missing cask, minus the one bag, to be returned. The French ships, which had already fought off three English cruisers were obliged to withdraw after vainly attempting to reclaim the now pointless gifts.

At about the same time news of the arrival of the gold, along with news of the Prince's flight to the Western Isles, reached the ears of the Prince's secretary, John Murray. Murray was convalescing in the company of another follower, Cameron of Lochiel, in a wood, close to Loch Arkaig. He hurried to Arisaig to take charge of the money, and made it his immediate task to provide for the wounded and the widows of the dead, allocating 500 *louis* in this way. He then had the rest of the money transferred to Loch Arkaig by Dr Archibald Cameron, Lochiel's brother, and returned there separately himself.

The New Uprising

On 8 May, many of the surviving Jacobite leaders met at Callich or Chailleach, on the shore of Loch Arkaig. Cameron of Lochiel, honoured in history as the 'gentle' Lochiel, presided, still limping from his wounds. As well as Murray, those present included the dauntless old rogue Lord Lovat, the excellent and loyal French officer,

Cameron of Lochiel, who owned Achnacarry House at the head of Loch Arkaig and left Scotland with his prince in September 1746, never to return.

Major Kennedy, who was Lochiel's uncle, the future traitor Barisdale, and the poet-soldier John Roy Stewart.

Encouraged by the French ships' arrival, they resolved upon a second uprising, intending to open with a gathering of the loyal clans at Glenmely, three miles from Lochiel's house, in ten days time (although this date was later put back one week). 600 *louis* were distributed to such as were commanders for future expenses, and a further 1,500 to cover various arrears.

Sometime within a week of the revised date of the uprising, probably on about 20 May, 15,000 of the *louis* were buried in three separate parcels of 5,000, each parcel containing five bags. One version of events, left by Murray in the statement of finances he later prepared, tells us that there was 'one parcel put under a rock in a small rivulet, the other two parcels in the ground at a little distance, the holes made and the money deposited by Sir Stewart Threpland, Mr Alexander McLeod yo[r] of Neuck, Major Kennedy, and Dr Cameron'. Elsewhere he says it was buried 'about

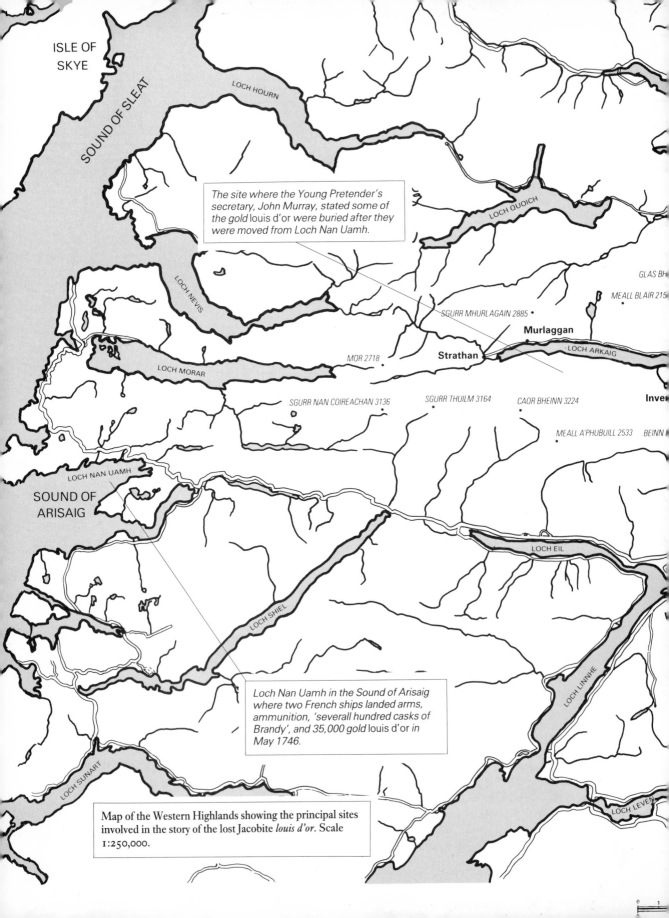

ISLE OF SKYE

SOUND OF SLEAT

LOCH HOURN

LOCH QUOICH

GLAS BH

MEALL BLAIR 215

LOCH NEVIS

SGURR MHURLAGAIN 2885 •

Murlaggan

The site where the Young Pretender's secretary, John Murray, stated some of the gold louis d'or were buried after they were moved from Loch Nan Uamh.

MOR 2718

Strathan

LOCH ARKAIG

LOCH MORAR

Inver

SGURR NAN COIREACHAN 3136

SGURR THUILM 3164

CAOR BHEINN 3224

MEALL A'PHUBUILL 2533

BEINN

LOCH NAN UAMH

SOUND OF ARISAIG

LOCH EIL

LOCH SHIEL

LOCH LINNHE

Loch Nan Uamh in the Sound of Arisaig where two French ships landed arms, ammunition, 'severall hundred casks of Brandy', and 35,000 gold louis d'or in May 1746.

LOCH SUNART

Map of the Western Highlands showing the principal sites involved in the story of the lost Jacobite *louis d'or*. Scale 1:250,000.

LOCH LEVEN

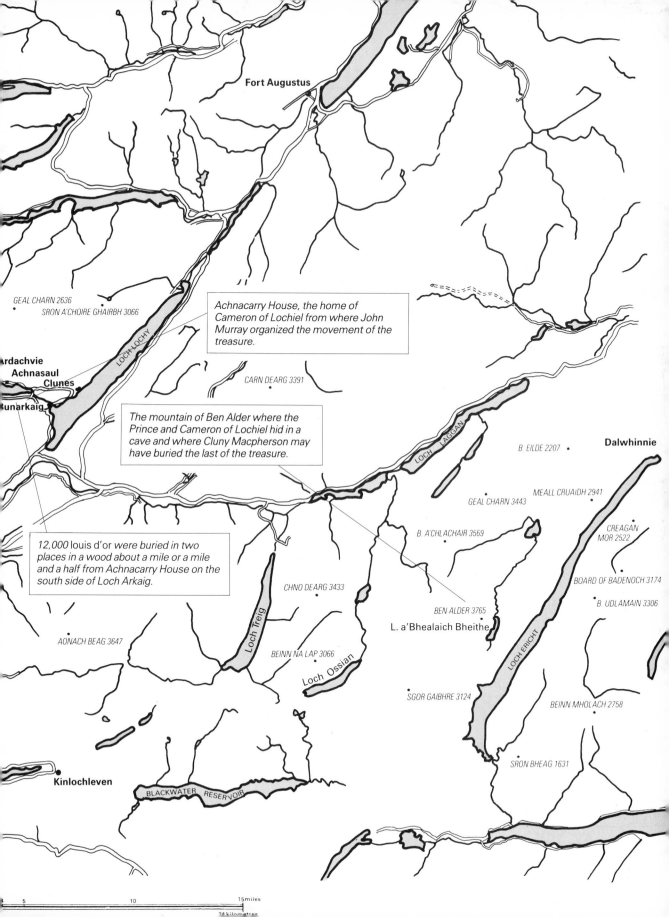

Fort Augustus

GEAL CHARN 2636
SRON A'CHOIRE GHAIRBH 3066

Achnacarry House, the home of
Cameron of Lochiel from where John
Murray organized the movement of the
treasure.

Ardachvie
Achnasaul
Clunes

CARN DEARG 3391

Bunarkaig

The mountain of Ben Alder where the
Prince and Cameron of Lochiel hid in a
cave and where Cluny Macpherson may
have buried the last of the treasure.

LOCH LAGGAN

B. EILDE 2207

Dalwhinnie

MEALL CRUAIDH 2941

GEAL CHARN 3443

CREAGAN
MOR 2522

B. A'CHLACHAIR 3569

12,000 louis d'or were buried in two
places in a wood about a mile or a mile
and a half from Achnacarry House on the
south side of Loch Arkaig.

BOARD OF BADENOCH 3174

B. UDLAMAIN 3306

CHNO DEARG 3433

BEN ALDER 3765

Loch Treig

L. a'Bhealaich Bheithe

AONACH BEAG 3647

BEINN NA LAP 3066

Loch Ossian

SGOR GAIBHRE 3124

BEINN MHOLACH 2758

Kinlochleven

SRON BHEAG 1631

BLACKWATER RESERVOIR

5   10   15miles

24 kilometres

Charles Edward Stuart, the Young Pretender. The French gold he left behind in Scotland became a permanent legacy of distrust and dishonesty among the clans.

south side of the Lake'.

After leaving their base, Murray and Lochiel set out with a number of followers to join other clans for the new uprising, but the English were about in strength and the little party was soon compelled to return to the head of the loch. There, they decided to disperse. As they were about to do so, a Donald Macleod came from the Prince to tell them he was hiding in South Uist and in want of brandy and money. In Macleod's own words, he 'got no money at all from Murray, who said he had none to give, having only about sixty *louis d'ores* to himself, which was not worth the while to send'.

At first sight, this seems ridiculous, but we must remember that the 12,000 *louis* were buried at the other end of the loch and were perhaps difficult or even dangerous to remove at short notice. In addition, Murray's own 5,000 may already have been exhausted and, most interestingly, he may not even have known precisely where the 15,000 *louis* at the head of the loch were buried. Against these possibilities, we must set some rather damning evidence. On the coast shortly afterwards, McDonald of Buisdale, who sought money from Murray in order to engage a ship for the Prince, was told 'that he [Murray] was surprised they had not mentioned that when at the head of Loch Arkike, where it was in his power to have given them any sum they could demand; but that now he had none alongst with him save a little for Common necessarys on the road'. The head of Loch Arkaig was, of course, just where Donald Macleod had met him.

Furthermore, if Murray's 5,000 *louis* really had been reduced to 60, how in the days ahead did he manage to find considerable sums to keep other Scots happy? Most notable were the 3,500 *louis* and 351 guineas deposited with Mrs Menzies of Culdairs.

Later, Murray answered the allegation 'that he refused to supply his Master when it was in his power' by giving an account of the meeting with McDonald (Murray, incidentally, never refers to Macleod's request). Murray concludes his defence by stressing that, *had he had money*, he would probably not have given it anyway, and he lists some sensible reasons: he had no confidence McDonald would find the Prince, he believed the

a mile and a half from the Loch on the west end of the south side of the lake in three places'. This was near the head of the Loch, opposite Callich.

The remainder of the money was carried around with them, including the emptied casks which were now filled with rocks, so that the other clans would not be offended by knowing of the trust Murray placed in the Camerons. Some of the time Murray stayed at Achnacarry House, the home of Lochiel, and it was from here, on the last night of their stay, that he ordered a further 12,000 *louis* to be buried, reserving about 5,000 for his own use. The French gold had been supplemented by nearly £3,000 from other sources, although Murray had also paid out several thousand. A *louis* was reckoned at £1. These *louis* were carried away by Dr Cameron and Alexander McLeod upon their shoulders and hidden in two places in the wood 'about a mile from Locheil's house at the foot of Loch Arkike'. Elsewhere, Murray tells us the locations were 'about a mile and a half from Lochiel's House, the

Prince already had plenty of money, he did not know if McDonald had authorization for his demand having nothing in writing to show for it, and finally he did not know if a proper account would be made of the arrangement, wishing in transactions with strangers to be as cautious as possible.

It seems reasonably clear, then, that Murray had withheld money, both from McDonald and Macleod, but for honourable reasons. His error was only in denying his possession of it, both then and later.

Murray's Capture

Murray headed southward after his meeting with McDonald on the coast, while Lochiel and Dr Cameron took refuge on Ben Alder where they were joined on 30 August by the Prince. Murray was captured by the English on Saturday 28 June, early in the morning while he slept in his sister's house in Peeblesshire: he had 95 guineas in his possession and was in poor health.

Almost at once Murray spilled the secret of the *louis d'or*. The Lord Justice Clerk wrote in the same month to the Duke of Newcastle about Murray's revelations, in which Murray feigned a vagueness as to the details of how the money was divided, excepting that 'he saved no more than what was now seized on him'.

On 13 August, Murray proved more amenable. He admitted to the caches of the 15,000 and the 12,000 *louis* and generously offered to lead the English to one of them. On 27 August he wrote a letter from the Tower to Andrew Stone, recently Under-Secretary of State, reminding him of the offer: 'Last time I had the honour to see you, I offered to lay my hand upon the 15,000 *louis d'or*, and am still certain I can do so, but as the season is now advancing, and the parties will probably soon be called in, it is not in that event impossible but the money may be raised [i.e. taken].'

The obvious inference is that Murray did not know where the 12,000 *louis* were to be found, and this would tally with his divergent statements that the 12,000 were 'about a mile' or 'about a mile and a half' from Achnacarry House. Insofar as Murray knew where part of the cache was, we would expect the English government to have

taken advantage of the information he offered, and therefore it is odd that the 15,000 *louis* were not quickly recovered under his guidance. It is clear that the English did not recover the money, but that the search may have been made without Murray's assistance.

If Murray did not know where the 12,000 *louis* were to be found, did he know about the 15,000 either? Murray's name does not figure in the lists of those responsible for the concealments, and, unless he had been present while Dr Cameron and his team had buried this first portion or had been taken to the site by one of the team afterwards, he could not know the exact location. His claim to know the location may well merely have been an attempt to gain bargaining power with the English government.

On about 1 September, Dr Cameron and Cluny Macpherson, another loyal Jacobite who had been hiding Cameron, Lochiel and for the last day or two the Prince as well on his estate, ventured back towards Loch Arkaig probably in order to remove some of the gold or to rebury it elsewhere. On the way they learned to their joy, from a certain Maccoilveen, that two ships, the *Princesse de Conti* and the *Heureux*, had arrived in Loch Nan Uamh on 6 September to take the Prince and his followers to France. Their mission was now forgotten, and, sending one Alexander Macpherson running on ahead with the news to take to the Prince, they turned back.

The Prince Departs

They arrived at Ben Alder very early in the morning on the 13th, to find the Prince already prepared for departure. They all set out at once, and on the morning of the 16th reached Achnacarry House, which the English had burned down in the meantime. On the night of the 16th, the Prince set out for Glencamger (perhaps now Glencamgarry), by Loch Arkaig, where he found Cluny and Dr Cameron waiting for him with a hearty meal they had gone to considerable

Overleaf: Ben Alder (from Sgor Gaibhre), where the French gold may have been buried by Cluny Macpherson and where the Prince sheltered in a cave after Culloden.

pains to prepare. On the 18th, the Prince set out at daylight from Glencamger and reached the place of anchorage on the following day. On the 20th, the Prince, Dr Cameron, Lochiel and about a hundred other loyalists took their leave of Scotland, some of them for the last time. Cluny Macpherson stayed behind, preferring a dangerous existence in his home country to life abroad. The guardianship of the gold now passed to him.

Did the Prince take any of the gold away with him? It would seem reasonable to suppose so both in view of Cluny's and Cameron's earlier un-named mission and the Prince's proximity to the gold just before boarding ship. Perhaps we should consider now the discoveries reported by an un-named English spy either in 1749 or early in the following year.

The spy had learned that Dr Cameron, with Major Kennedy and Alexander McLeod, had hidden all the gold 'underground in the head of Locharkick, in the middle of a Wood'. These three, along with Sir Stewart Threpland, had of course not hidden all the gold but just the 15,000 *louis*. The spy had also heard, more interestingly, how English troops had 'afterwards search'd the woods of Locharkick for this money, and were often round the place where it was, and missed very narrowly finding it, for being hid by Gentle-men, not used to work, it was very unskilfully done, and the stamps and impressions of their feet visible about the place. But as soon as Dr Camer-on found a proper opportunity, he went and took up the money and hid it elsewhere in the wood.'

This may very well be true. Since 13 August, the English had known about the hiding-places and are likely to have attempted a search—especially after Murray's warning on the 27th that the money might soon be taken. Given the search, or even the threat of one following Murray's cap-ture, it would have been natural for Dr Cameron to try to move the money. He is most likely to have done this just before the journey to France.

The spy, whose facts are garbled at some points, would place Dr Cameron's removal of the gold earlier than I would. He says, talking of events im-mediately before the journey to France, only that Cameron showed Cluny the two caches, nor does he claim to know if anything was taken abroad.

'But Certain it is,' he continues, 'that Cluny immediately after [i.e. the ship's departure] Car-ried the £12,000 to Badenoch...'. and 'The other part of the money ... he either did not find an opportunity or did not think convenient to come for it, until a month afterwards, when he came and carried it also away'. The spy reports the general and accurate belief that the total was between £20,000 and £30,000. He also names or identifies those who helped Cluny make the first removal. The *louis d'or*, now amounting to £27,000 or a little less if the Prince took some on board, were taken to Cluny Macpherson's estate. Since he himself continued living for part of the time in Ben Alder, in one or other of the caves, we may be right to assume the gold was hidden somewhere close to that mountain: it was dangerous for him to go any distance, and he had to keep an eye on his charge.

The Prince Across the Water

Our records are almost silent about Cluny and the treasure for the next two and a half years. An anonymous note of 26 January 1748 lifts the veil for a moment: 'Scyphax is still in the country and there are disturbances between him and the Dorians and Aetolians over the goods left by the Young Mogul ... Nothing but stealing and plundering prevails in all quarters here.' These erudite references are said to be, in order, to Cluny, the Camerons of Gleneavis, the Glengarrys, and the Prince. Cluny, in honouring his trust to the Prince, had been making enemies of those less scrupulous than himself, and this is confirmed later by the English spy. Amongst other charges levelled at the time, Cameron of Gleneavis, whose brother helped Cluny remove the £12,000, is said to have become suddenly rich after being almost bankrupt. His brother, Angus, is also said to have taken £2,500.

In February of the following year, the Prince wrote to Major Kennedy, who was living in London, to ask him to arrange with Cluny via a friend in Northumberland to transmit part of the treasure. But things did not go according to plan, and we find the Prince writing from Strasbourg to a Mr Waters on 6 April: 'You may let Mr Newton [i.e. Major Kennedy] know that whenever he has thoroly finished his Business, Mr Williams [i.e. The Prince] will make him very wellcum in all his Cuntrihouses'.

This reminder also failed to have any effect and on 30 April the Prince wrote again expressing 'his surprise and impatience for the delay of the horses [i.e. money] and other goods promised by Mr Newton'. In the spring or early summer, Major Kennedy was imprisoned by the English and questioned in London by the Duke of Newcastle, who was particularly interested in the details relating to the treasure. Kennedy gave nothing away and, on his release shortly afterwards, crossed over to Paris to give an account of himself before returning to England, still with the intention of taking the treasure to the Prince.

In August, Kennedy wrote that Cluny could do nothing until winter 'on account of the sheilings'. These summer homes of the pastoral Highlanders were evidently situated too close to the cache for comfort. So the waiting went on.

The Treachery of Young Glengarry

At last, removals from the cache began to be made, but not by Major Kennedy. The young Glengarry, a member of one of the families who had been in dispute with Cluny for a long time about the treasure, seems to have taken away up to £2,000 for his own use. Although part of this— £1,200 according to Lord Elcho—came from Cluny's cache, the rest came from a part of Murray's £5,000 mysteriously secreted in Edinburgh, in contradiction to Murray's own statements on the subject. This disgraceful theft, following the earlier charge against Cameron of Gleneavis, was the last straw. Dissension grows steadily worse from this point.

At the beginning of the following year, Major Kennedy was complaining of Cluny's delaying tactics, while the young Glengarry was trying to put the blame for the theft on Dr Cameron who had returned to Scotland during the winter and had also taken some money for legitimate purposes. Some of the squabblers, including the young Glengarry and Dr Cameron, went to Rome in the spring, probably in order to sort the matter out before the Prince's father, the Old Pretender. Nothing, of course, was sorted out.

Nonetheless the Prince's father should have been able to draw his own conclusions after learning that the young Glengarry had forged an authorization from him, complete with bogus signature, to obtain the money at Edinburgh. Glengarry was also later responsible for a bogus statement of Cluny's accounts, exonerating himself and incriminating others. Unhappily, the young Glengarry managed to damn Dr Cameron in many eyes including Major Kennedy's. However, the good Major may have been correct when he wrote in March: 'C [Cluny] in my opinion is more to be blamed than any of them, for if he had a mind to act the honest part he certainly could have given up the whole long since'. Kennedy noted in the same letter that Dr Cameron, Glengarry and several others too had been 'very flush of money' lately. His report must be taken seriously, though it is probably inaccurate with regard to Dr Cameron.

Mud will stick, however, and it was widely believed that Dr Cameron had helped himself to 6,000 *louis d'or*, a small fortune. Even Kennedy was not free from suspicion, and was accused by the cowardly banker, Aeneas Macdonald, of squandering £800 backing losing horses at Newmarket with money obtained from Cluny. By June of 1750, an honest cousin of Glengarry's named Lochgarry was writing that he had recently seen Cluny, who had complained of the money 'torn from him' so that he had no more than 16,000 *louis d'or* remaining. Lochgarry wished to be commissioned with Dr Cameron to rescue the remaining sum, but nothing came of this.

The following year, Glengarry wrote to tell the Prince of his approaching marriage to a lady from a good English family, after which he would be happy to repay his share of the treasure—so transparently admitting to his theft. He was living publicly in London at that time and indeed had nothing to fear from the English government, for it seems that he had already acquired his new identity as the spy, Pickle—an identity not discovered until more than a century after his death.

In 1753, Dr Cameron made one final attempt to retrieve the gold for the Prince. He crossed over from France, but his luck did not hold and on 12 March he was captured at Glenbucket,

The treacherous young Glengarry who stole from the French gold and probably betrayed Dr Cameron. He died in 1761, his identity as an English spy still hidden from the world.

betrayed to the English, it would seem, by Glengarry. Soon after, he was brought to trial for treason and hanged at Tyburn, after many vain appeals, on 7 June, the last Jacobite to suffer so. He won all hearts by his gentle manner, cheerfulness and the courage he displayed to the last moment. If any had doubted his honesty, he left behind a family utterly destitute. After the hanging, rumours circulated that the English were still after the secret of the gold, which Dr Cameron had refused them. But it is more likely that they believed he was involved in plans for a further

An account of the capture of the gallant Dr Archibald Cameron, who was executed in 1753, the last Jacobite to die for the Young Pretender's cause.

uprising, and was acting as an emissary to Frederick of Prussia.

In September of the following year, the Prince, desperately in need of money, wrote 'in great straits' to Cluny. He summoned him to Paris and requested him to bring over 'all the effects whatsoever that I left in your hands, also whatever money you can come at'. Undoubtedly, his eye was mainly upon the remains of the gold, but perhaps also he hoped for contributions from sympathizers, the nominal object of Dr Cameron's visit the previous year.

Cluny set off to France within a few weeks, so ending his uncomfortable and disheartening eight-year vigil. We do not know what he took with him, but he is commonly believed, probably in view of the supposed large quantity remaining, to have left much behind. The latest estimate of this quantity, made in June 1750 by Cluny himself, gives a figure of 16,000 *louis d'or*. We know of no depletions, honourable or dishonourable, after that date until Cluny's departure to France. It is likely therefore that he had a sum close to this figure to draw from.

FURTHER ACTION

What he did not take with him we would expect to find somewhere in the neighbourhood of the mountain, Ben Alder, where for part of the time he was living. Chambers, the historian, tells us his chief residence was 'in a cave near the site of his destroyed house'. This is presumably not the same as Cluny's remote 'Cage', the rough shelter he built himself, where the Prince and Lochiel had sheltered for a time. The latter was to be found 'in the face of a very rough, high, rocky mountain called Letternilichk, which is still a part of Benalder, full of great stones and crevices, and some scattered wood interspersed'. Like the cave near the house, it must have been used sometimes by Cluny during his years of concealment.

Our only other clue is the reference to the shielings, which prevented Cluny's access to the treasure in the summer of 1749. The country around Ben Alder was, according to the historian Chambers, 'destitute of wood; but it made up for the deficiency as a place of concealment by the rockiness of its hills and glens'. I believe Cluny hid the treasure, probably near one of the caves, from where he could not transfer it far without being seen. We may leave the last word with the son of the Old Pretender's secretary, Edgar, writing sadly to his father after Dr Cameron's capture: 'I wish with all my heart the Gov. had got it [the gold] in the beginning, for it has given the greatest stroke to the cause that can be imagined, it has divided the different clans more than ever, and even those of the same clan and family; so that they are ready to destroy and betray one another.'

COCOS ISLAND, COSTA RICA, EAST PACIFIC

BONITO'S HOARD AND LIMA GOLD

Four hundred miles off the coast of Colombia, in South America lies the most romantic island in the world, a tiny speck of land, lonely, uninhabited, set like a green jewel in the blue vastness of the Southern Pacific ... it rises from the sea, a green mountainous steep, crowned by twin peaks and walled by ramparts of unscaleable rock ...

So Sir Malcolm Campbell, 'speed-king' and treasure hunter, mixing his metaphors in lyrical over-enthusiasm, introduced the world's most famous treasure site, the probable model for Robert Louis Stevenson's *Treasure Island.*

Cocos (to be distinguished from the Cocos or Keeling Islands in the Indian Ocean) has an area of about ten square miles. It is roughly twice as long as it is wide. Its bearings are 5° 32' N, 87° 10' W. It owes its name to the coconut trees which grow on its principal rocky plateau amidst almost impenetrable rain-forest vegetation. Three great volcanic peaks arise above this plateau. The highest is Mount Iglesia at 1,932 ft. Chatham and Wafer, in the north, are its two principal bays. Both are suitable for shipping and have fresh water springs.

Although it has had a few settlers from time to time, it is now inhabited only by a 'garrison' of three Costa Rican soldiers who live on the beach at Wafer Bay. Cocos may look like a 'green jewel'. It is, in fact, an inhospitable hell-hole. In summer the heat is oppressive. Temperatures of 115 °F are common and humidity intense. In the winter, rain falls steadily and heavily for weeks on end. The dense vegetation and the steep rocky slopes make any movement into the interior both difficult and dangerous, and the swarms of insects are inescapable. Cocos is not a place to live. It is a place to visit briefly. It is because people have visited it briefly and then sailed away throughout history that we are concerned with it today.

Pirate headquarters

The island makes its first appearance on a French map by Nicolas Desliens in 1541. Many pirates were amongst its earliest visitors. Captain Edward Davis used the island as his headquarters at the end of the seventeenth century. He is said to have buried several chests of treasure, which he landed at Chatham Bay.

John Eaton, Captain of the *Nicholas* of London left a record of a visit to the island in the course of his privateering. 'The middle of the island is pretty high, and destitute of trees, but looks green and pleasant with a herb called by the Spaniards *Gramadiel*. All round the island by the sea the land is low, and there coconut trees grow in great grooves.' The rank vegetation there is a new phenomenon. As late as 1838, an English captain could report (in contradiction of other accounts) 'the thicket is not now impenetrable'.

In the eighteenth century, the island found occasional use as a watering place and source of fresh food. In 1795, an officer in the Royal Navy, George Vancouver, who was surveying the North Pacific on the Admiralty's orders, paid a call to the island. As well as a message hanging in a bottle from a tree in which a Lieutenant James Colnett had recorded his visit two years before, he saw the pigs, now wild, which Colnett had left behind. Descendants of these are still to be found on the island.

His men struggled to make sense of the in-

Cocos Island, far to the west of Colombia, for centuries provided a haven for pirates. The story of the largest treasure believed to have been hidden there tells of

Spanish wealth removed from Lima in 1820 at the time of the South American wars of independence.

scriptions carved by its former visitors on the rocks of Chatham Bay. In particular, they could not agree on the meaning of one poorly executed and much defaced inscription '*Look Y. as you goe for ye I. Coco*'. This inscription included four branched crosses. It is difficult to see what this can refer to. Have we here our earliest indication of the presence of treasure? Or was it merely a kind-hearted mariner's attempt to indicate that coconuts were only to be had in the bay adjacent?

Benito Bonito

Another pirate with whom the island is associated is Benito Bonito. Of uncertain nationality, Bonito first plied his trade in the rich hunting-grounds of the Caribbean. When the British navy made things too hot for him, he rounded Cape Horn and resumed his trade in the Pacific. Between

1818 and 1820 he commanded his ship *Relampago* in a series of attacks on treasure galleons and coastal towns in Central America.

In 1819, he made his greatest coup. He heard of a large shipment of treasure bound for Manila. As the mule-train trudged from Mexico City to Acapulco, Bonito and his men fell upon it and seized an enormous hoard. It is said that this was taken to the island and buried under the cliffs of Wafer Bay.

This account surfaced in 1853 when John and Mary Welch came to San Francisco. Mary claimed to have been Bonito's mistress. She is our authority for identifying him with a former English naval officer named Bennet Graham. His nickname would thus have been no more than a complimentary Latinization. 'Pretty' or 'good-looking' Bennet. On the strength of her story, which is elaborate in its detail right down to

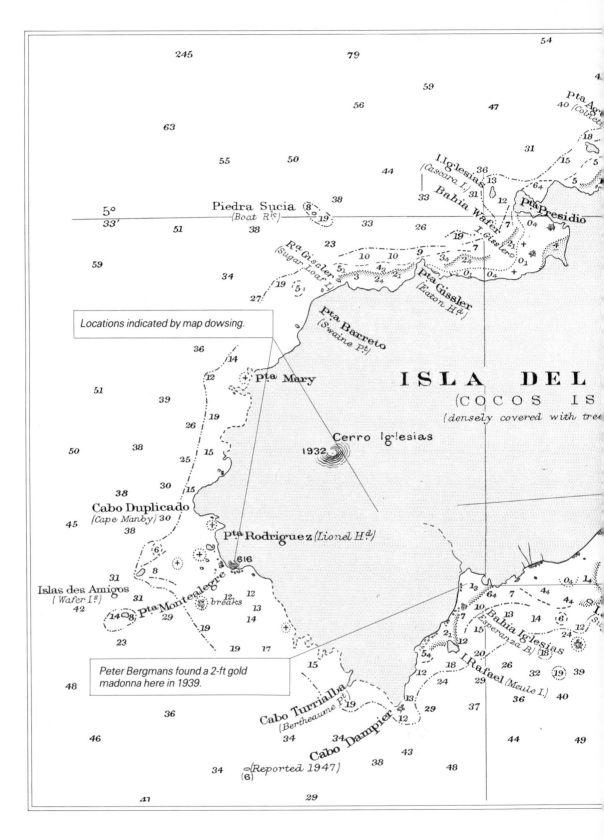

245   79   54

59

56   47   Pta Ag
40 (Colnett)

63   18

31   15

55   50   44   I. Iglesias   36
(Cascara I.)   13   64   5
33   31   12   PtaPresidio

5°   Piedra Sucia (8   Bahia Wafer   7   0.4
33'   (Boat Rk)   19   33   26   19   7
51   38   I. Gissler   4

23
59   Ra Gissler   10   10   9   24
(Sugar Loaf I.)   5.   4.   3.   0.4
34   3   2.   Pta Gissler   0.1
27   19   5   (Eaton Hd)   0.4

Locations indicated by map dowsing.   Pta Barreto
(Swaine Pt)

36   14   ISLA   DEL
12   Pta Mary   (COCOS   IS
51   39   19   (densely covered with tree

26   Cerro Iglesias
38   15   1932
50   25   15
30   15
38   Cabo Duplicado
45   (Cape Manby) 30   Pta Rodriguez (Lionel Hd)
38
6   616   1.3   64   7   44
31   8   10   13   14   6
Islas des Amigos   7   13   15   Bahia Iglesias   24   12
(Wafer Is)   31   Pta Montealegre   12   12   20   (Esperanza B)   18
42   14   8   29   breaks   13   2.   54   26   19   39
23   19   14   18   32
Peter Bergmans found a 2-ft gold   15   12   24   29   I.Rafael   36   40
madonna here in 1939.   29   (Meule I.)
48   37   44   49
36   Cabo Turrialba   19   13   29
(Bertheaume Pt)   12
46   34   Cabo Dampier   43
34   (Reported 1947)   38   48
(6)
41   29

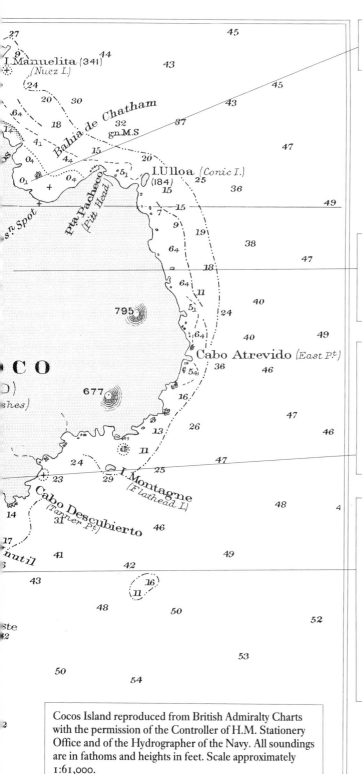

A gold chain was found here in 1948 by James Forbes, a descendant of Captain Thompson's First Mate.

Captain Thompson's instructions, as given by Keating to Fitzgerald in 1868 (and quoted on p. 67), led to a point in the north of the island. Keating seems to have discovered the treasure and moved it to different places in the south.

Keating's own instructions for part of the hoard are: 'Disembark in the Bay of Hope between two islets in water five fathoms deep. Walk 350 paces along the course of the stream then turn NNE for 850 yards—stake—setting sun—stake—draws silhouette of an eagle with wings spread: At the extremity of the sun and shadow: cave marked with a cross. Here lies the treasure.'

Keating's notes from one of his searches indicate another location at the Bay of Hope. 'At two cables lengths, south of the last watering place, on three points. The cave is the one which is to be found under the second point.

Christie, Ned and Anton have tried but none of the three has returned. Ned on his fourth dive found the entrance at twelve fathoms but did not emerge from his fifth dive.

There are no octopuses but there are sharks.

A path must be opened up to the cave from the west. I believe there has been a fall of rock at the entrance.'

Cocos Island reproduced from British Admiralty Charts with the permission of the Controller of H.M. Stationery Office and of the Hydrographer of the Navy. All soundings are in fathoms and heights in feet. Scale approximately 1:61,000.

Bonito's capture, trial and hanging, and Mary's transportation to Tasmania, a company was formed by some wealthy businessmen to recover the treasure.

Mary's maps proved useless. Once on the island, she said that everything had changed in the intervening years. She could no longer recognize the treasure site. They dug extensively but found nothing.

The *Mary Dear*, Thompson and Forbes

The elusive story of the Cocos Island treasure moves onto firmer ground with the story of the *Mary Dear*. In 1820, the revolutionary troops of Simon Bolivar, under General San Martin and Lord Cochrane, were approaching Lima, then considered the richest island on the continent. The richer Spanish inhabitants of Lima resolved on flight. This was only possible by sea, and there was only one vessel fit for the crossing to Spain, the *Esmeralda*, but this was under express orders to defend Callao, Lima's port. A Scottish captain, William Thompson, also had his ship, the *Mary Dear*, in harbour and was about to remove himself from the imminent battle. He was persuaded, at a price, to take aboard the wealthy citizens and all their most precious possessions, including a life-size statue of the Virgin from Lima Cathedral made from pure gold and encrusted with jewels. According to contemporary sources this alone weighed over a ton.

Although the exact versions are lost and we can take our choice of a number of different versions, Thompson seems to have succumbed to the temptation which the vast riches offered. Whether he left his passengers behind on shore or murdered them in their cabins, he certainly succeeded in ridding himself of them and made for Cocos Island, where the treasure was at once buried.

What happened after that is uncertain, but Thompson and his crew were captured, and all but himself and his First Mate, believed to be one

The capture of *The Esmeralda*, the flagship of the Spanish Pacific Fleet, by Lord Cochrane on 5 November 1820 at Lima's heavily fortified port, Callao. A few days before,

Captain William Thompson set sail with a group of Lima's wealthy citizens and a cargo of their possessions.

James Alexander Forbes, were hanged. These two men were temporarily spared for the sake of the secret they possessed and succeeded in escaping when they were brought back to Cocos under armed guard in a bid to recover the treasure.

The Spaniards searched fruitlessly in the thick undergrowth and in the following months sent two ships to recover the fugitives. Thompson and his mate were at last rescued from Cocos by an English whaler, *Captain*, who accepted their story of shipwreck. The whaler took them to Puntarenas on the Costa Rican coast.

Thompson reappeared in 1841. He had never returned to the island, but, crossing from the West Indies to Newfoundland told his story to a friend, John Keating. They remained friends on shore and, either then or on his deathbed three years later, Thompson gave Keating a map pinpointing the treasure, with a letter of instructions. These instructions, for which Chatham Bay should be taken as the starting point, are as follows:

> Turn your back on the sea and then make your way towards the mountain that is in the north of the island. On the mountain slope you will see a brook to the west. Cross this and go twenty more paces due west. Then take fifty paces towards the centre of the island until the sea is completely hidden behind the mountain. At the place where the ground suddenly falls away you will see a white mark on the rock. That is where the cave is. It has a well hidden entrance covered by a stone slab and the tunnel entrance leads sideways into a chamber.

Keating's Search

Keating, agog with excitement, found a backer for his proposed expedition and in about 1844 set off with a certain Captain Boag. Arriving in Chatham Bay, Keating and Boag went ashore without the other members of the crew and had no trouble in locating the cache.

What met their eyes astonished them by its richness. They decided to tell the rest of the crew nothing and take just what they could carry in their pockets. But the others, who had already learned the reason for the voyage, would not believe them when they said they had failed in their search. Under threats they confessed and agreed to go in a party to the cave the following morning. That same night, they slipped over the side and went into hiding in the dense jungle.

For several days, the others hunted for them, but at last they gave up and sailed away. When a ship called in for water several months later, only Keating was alive. He claimed that Boag had accidentally drowned.

There is another, rather different version of Keating's discovery. This states that Keating and Boag (or Boeck as his name is spelled here) set sail for Cocos in 1846 on the brigantine *Edgecombe* under the command of a certain Captain Gould. The captain, so the story goes, got wind of what the two men were after and demanded a share of the treasure for himself. As in the first version, they escaped by running off into the jungle in much the same way as Thompson and *his* mate had done years earlier.

Be that as it may there is some reason for believing that Keating murdered Boag while they were on the island, and indeed, back in Newfoundland an attempt was made to charge him with the murder. The indictment failed for lack of evidence. A later friend of his, Nicholas Fitzgerald, recorded his unwillingness to accompany Keating to the island, for 'I thought I would be running grave risk of my life to go single-handed with him. This disappearance of Boag was unsatisfactorily explained to me by him ...'

Nicholas Fitzgerald

Fitzgerald also says that in making conditions for an expedition Keating insisted 'that I should enter the cave alone, as he had pledged himself never again to enter it. I attribute that to fear of something'. Was it Boag's corpse, left where Keating had trapped him, which Keating was so loath to encounter? Keating evidently returned home with some of the treasure, buying business property in St. John's and a farm. He made another expedition to Cocos Island, in which there was a second mutiny, and he was again obliged to hide. After fourteen days' diet of ground roots, he got taken off by whalers, again with some gold concealed about him.

1868 found him in Codroy Village, on the western coast of Newfoundland. He had been shipwrecked, journeying in a schooner owned by himself that was lost in the ice. 'He was in great distress on account of the loss of his vessel and want of provisions for himself and crew, and he was also sick and living for the time in an old deserted house, sleeping in a vessel's sail lying on the floor, banked with ice and snow.' Nicholas Fitzgerald helped him at this time (it is his account that is quoted here), and Keating entrusted the secret of the treasure to Fitzgerald as an act of gratitude. Fitzgerald inherited from Keating not only the instructions of Thompson's already given, but another set, which may lead to a portion of Thompson's treasure removed by Keating from its original hiding-place.

The Herald newspaper of Sydney, Nova Scotia on the first of December 1880, however, carries an official notice in which Keating declares that he has passed on all the relevant documents and information about the treasure to one Thomas Hackett. Keating goes out of his way to state that neither Richard Young (his son-in-law) *nor anyone else* has information which will enable him to find the treasure.

Richard Young did actually try to raise capital for an expedition on the strength of knowledge gleaned from his father-in-law, but unsuccessfully. As for Thomas Hackett it is thought that he died before being able to use the knowledge. The information and documents then passed to his brother Captain Fred M. Hackett whom we shall meet presently.

To return to Fitzgerald however, he had declined a partnership with Keating, and could

An old wreck in Chatham Bay.

Left: Chatham Bay, the principal anchorage off Cocos Island, has figured prominently amongst the Cocos treasure sites. Here, in the 1960s, four French students found a cave containing much gold.

Right: August Gissler was a German who came to live on Cocos Island in 1891. Despite his possession of treasure maps and extensive searching, all he found was a few coins and a few artefacts.

not afford to prepare an expedition by himself. In 1894, he wrote a letter to Commodore Curzon-Howe whom he knew of as an honourable man and who was occasionally on duty in the Pacific. He was trying to set up a deal whereby, in return for the secret, he would receive a twentieth-share of the gross value of the cave's contents. This came to nothing, but they exchanged several letters, in which Fitzgerald passed on all that he knew.

Later Expeditions

Meanwhile, Cocos Island, thanks not least to Mary Welch, was attracting a regular flow of visitors. There have probably been several hundred attempts to find the Cocos treasures. Most have returned empty-handed.

One man who must be singled out is the German sailor, August Gissler. His interest in Cocos began when he met a young Portuguese named Manoel Cabral on the *Highflyer* sailing from London to Honolulu. Cabral's grandfather had been taken prisoner by pirates while fishing

off the Azores. Gissler read and copied the grandfather's long account of his sea-journeys. Eventually, it said, he helped Bonito to hide two hoards of treasure near a waterfall on Cocos.

On his arrival in Honolulu, Gissler met an old sailor named Mac who lived near Pagola. Mac claimed to have sailed with Bonito and also possessed a Spanish treasure map. The island on the map was named as 'Las Palmas' and lay at 5° 27′ N, 87° 0′ W. Gissler compared the two sets of evidence and concluded that the island must indeed be Cocos.

After several fruitless expeditions, Gissler received permission in June 1891 to found a colony at Wafer Bay. The Costa Rican government also gave him another treasure map which confirmed his opinion that the treasure lay near the coast. Although Gissler became the island's most knowledgeable and notable inhabitant and at length brought his own family and several others to live with him there, his ten or more years of search yielded nothing more than a number of rusty tools and a few gold coins.

The inheritance from Keating, as will be seen,

is complicated. I have already referred to the two sets of instructions received by Fitzgerald. Keating's widow possessed directions and a map, although Fitzgerald says her map was of no use without the instructions which only he possessed, and there was also a third set. These are not from Thompson, but are Keating's own notes, presumably made on his second expedition, which run as follows:

At two cables lengths, south of the last watering-place, on three points. The cave is the one which is to be found under the second point.

Christie, Ned and Anton have tried but none of the three has returned. Ned on his fourth dive found the entrance at twelve fathoms but did not emerge from his fifth dive.

There are no octopuses but there are sharks.

A path must be opened up to the cave from the west. I believe there has been a fall of rock at the entrance.

Wafer Bay, where Gissler founded his colony. The little 'garrison' of Costa Rican soldiers who police the island now live here.

These notes are preserved in the Nautical and Traveller's Club in Sydney, registered under No. 18,755, where they were copied by Captain Tony Mangel in 1927. Mangel made two visits to Cocos Island, the first in the same year that he saw the documents, the second in 1929 when he returned alone. 'I came back to Cocos Island in 1929,' he wrote later. 'This time I came well prepared, with shovels, pickaxes and dynamite. Best of all, I had studied Thompson's indications in terms of degree and minutes ... indications which I alone possessed. Of one thing I was certain as a result of this—these indications were false. And that is where the secret lay!

'They were false because we were now in the twentieth century and therefore working with a sextant and other very accurate instruments which took into account the declination of the compass. Thompson, on the other hand, had hidden his treasure in 1820 and 1823; his watch, however, was only relatively accurate and his compass pointed to a well-determined magnetic north. Thompson's calculations would have to be made all over again, repeating the same mistakes and using data from the nautical tables of the years between 1820 and 1823. Corrected in this way, the point I obtained in 1929 was the following: 5° 30' 17" latitude N and 87° 0' 40" longitude W.

Within a hundred yards of that spot lay the treasure.'

These bearings took him in 1929 to a spot south of the Bay of Hope, NNE of Meule Island (also called Rafael) where he found a cave only accessible briefly at low tide.

'At that spot and on that particular day the current was very strong. I had anchored my yacht and let my dinghy slip at the end of a rope right down to the back of the cave where a small sandbank rose from the water. In the semi-darkness I began to probe the sand—and then to dig with the shovel, for about three feet down I had felt a resistance which led me to hope there might be something there.'

Tony Mangel did not find the treasure, but he was very close to it, all the same. Two years later, a Belgian, Peter Bergmans, using the information Mangel had provided, found in the Bay of Hope a 2-ft gold madonna, which he afterwards sold for $11,000 in New York. Bergmans, in a cave different from Mangel's, claims to have found chests full of gold and a human skeleton. It strains credibility to learn that he touched none of this treasure and, like Bob Flower, could never get back to it.

Many twentieth-century tourists and treasure

hunters visited Cocos. Sir Malcolm Campbell arrived in 1926 on his yacht and spent several days there with his friends following up some clues derived, *via* Commodore Curzon-Howe's son, from Fitzgerald. 'The heat was terrific and the bugs bit all the time. Our faces and necks were livid with bites and scratches and the perspiration poured off us, until our Khaki drill shorts and shirts clung limply to our bodies as wet as though we had just come soaked out of the stream.' He found nothing but a spade and an old rig-bolt.

Franklin D. Roosevelt was another of the many interested visitors who briefly searched for treasure and found nothing on Cocos. A few finds have been claimed, including the almost certainly fallacious 'hoard of gold' found by a Colonel Leckie in 1932 and, equally dubiously, the 123 gold and silver coins 'discovered' by a Captain Bellamy. In 1948, an American named Forbes, a descendant of the man claimed to be Thompson's first mate, found a length of beautiful gold chain in the sand near the creek which flows into Chatham Bay. Forbes maintains that, near the mouth of the creek, there is a cache which is underwater at high tide.

Success

The only truly successful visit to the island in recent years was by Jacques Boucaud, a French student, and three young companions who arrived on Cocos in 1966. Boucaud had read of the treasure in a magazine article by a Canadian searcher who had failed to persuade the Costa Ricans to allow him to stay long enough to conduct a proper search. After two years of preparation and intensive research, therefore, Boucaud and his team resolved to conduct their own search illegally. Learning from the mistakes of others they equipped themselves against the exigencies of the climate and with a range of specialized mechanical and electronic equipment. Their expedition was a model of efficiency and self-reliance, in marked contrast to the many dilatory and disorderly affairs of the 1930s. For each of the two treasures they concluded that there were three possible sites. Having posted a look-out and found a suitable cave near a waterfall for their equipment, they started to work through these sites one by one. They started with Fitzgerald's directions to the treasures of Lima. From the north-east part of the island, it said ...

> Follow the coastline of the bay till you find a creek where, at high-water mark, you go up the bed of a stream which flows inland. Now you step out seventy paces, west by south, and against the skyline you will see the gap in the hills. From any other point, the gap is invisible. Turn north and walk to a stream. You will see a hole large enough for you to insert your thumb. Thrust in an iron bar, twist it round in the cavity, and behind you will find a door which opens on the treasure.

Another account agrees with this.

> We anchored in a bay and landed on a sandy beach where a small stream runs out. Stretching back from the beach is a piece of level ground about two acres

One of the most entertaining and unusual characters in the pageant of treasure-seekers at Cocos was Peter Bergmans, a Belgian, who, in 1931, found a 2 ft. gold madonna in the Bay of Hope. Bergmans also claimed to know of a treasure on the mainland but was unable or unwilling to lead a party, for whom he was acting as guide, back to it.

in extent. We followed the stream and, near its head at the foot of a hill, on a piece of level ground, we selected a spot where we hid the treasure.

The Frenchmen concluded that the bay must be Chatham. They found the cleft in the hills, the steep rock all but concealed by thick vegetation, and even the niche in the rock face. They levered out the slab of stone and found themselves in the empty cave where they had already been living for some days. Perhaps, then, one of the pirates or treasure hunters who had been marooned on Cocos had more success than he had revealed. The students continued to search for caves. On the fourth day, René, one of the party, found a new cave on the slope of a hill shown on their map as being 50 yards from Cabo Atrevida on the Eastern side of the island. Two human skeletons lay in this cave. One, whose back was to the cave wall, still clasped the hasp of an axe. The other lay in a heap on his right side with a large hole in his skull. There were traces of hair still visible on both skulls. Beyond this grisly montage, the Frenchmen found two pick-axes, two crowbars, an oil lamp, various crocks and kettles, a heap of carefully folded jute sacks and some wooden boxes without locks. Two bush knives and two muskets lay over the sacks. The back of the cave was a smooth steep wall.

Charles, the medical student of the party, examined the two skeletons. The men appeared to have killed one another. The cleft in the skull of one seemed consistent with an axe-blow. The man was tentatively said to have been in his mid-twenties at the time of his death. He wore a gold cross inlaid with mother of pearl, a pocket watch on a heavy gold chain, a heavy leather belt with a silver buckle and a gold ring engraved '*A. R. 15. 3. 41.*' His leather scabbard was mounted with the initials GLML. The other skeleton (of a man estimated to have been about thirty at death) was similarly, though less richly dressed and a knife was found amongst his ribs.

The sea chests all had the initials GM or WS burned into their lids. In the first, they found clothing, an English Bible printed in Boston in 1840, a leather-bound third volume of Captain George Vancouver's *A Voyage of Discoveries to the North Pacific Ocean and Around the Globe* (London,

1798). On the fly-leaf were the words '*Property of Gerald MacIntosh*'. Below these were rolls of tobacco, a compass, a small wooden sewing-casket and a quadrant, a revolver wrapped in leather and a leather bag. The bag contained nearly a thousand Spanish gold coins and, laid beneath a shirt, fifteen long gold bars weighing approximately half a pound apiece.

The second case contained similar personal baggage, another thousand gold coins in a similar bag, another fifteen of the rough gold bars and a Maryland newspaper cutting which might just be supposed to identify WS. It offers a 50-dollar reward for the capture of a runaway negro slave named William in Maryland. Amongst other finds was a board on which someone had painstakingly inscribed the words '*THE Bird is* '.

The students smuggled their gold back to France stitched into their rucksacks or concealed in their oxygen cylinders. We can only speculate as to whether the two skeletons were those of men who had found treasure or of men who were about to bury it. The 1840 volume and the revolver clearly prove that they had nothing to do with the fugitives from Lima. Even if they had found treasure from the Lima ship, however, perhaps in the cave which the students first found, there is still wealth enough on Cocos to justify continued searching. Among the documents that Fitzgerald passed to Curzon-Howe was an inventory which ran:

We have buried at a depth of four feet in red earth
1 chest: altar trimmings of cloth of gold, with baldachins, monstrances, chalices, comprising 1,244 stones.
1 chest: 2 gold reliquaries weighing 120 pounds, with 624 topazes, cornelians and emeralds, 12 diamonds.
1 chest: 3 reliquaries of cast metal weighing 160 pounds, with 860 rubies and various stones, 19 diamonds.
1 chest: 4,000 doubloons of Spain marked *8*, 5,000 crowns of Mexico, 124 swords, 64 dirks, 120 shoulder belts, 28 rondaches [small shields].
1 chest: 8 caskets of cedar wood and silver, with 3,840 cut stones, rings, patens and 4,265 uncut stones.
28 feet to the north-east at a depth of eight feet in the yellow sand.

7 chests with 22 candelabra in gold and silver, weighing 250 pounds, and 164 rubies.

12 armspans west, at a depth of ten feet in the red earth.

The seven-foot Virgin of gold with the child Jesus and her crown and pectoral of 780 pounds, rolled in her gold chasuble on which are 1,684 jewels. Three of these are four-inch emeralds on the pectoral and six are six-inch topazes on the crown. The seven crosses are of diamonds.

FURTHER ACTION

Cocos defies random on site searching, although many of the stories suggest that thorough and detailed research of the relevant texts and of the conditions will yield results. Our primary source is Keating, and, through him, Fitzgerald (though the Forbes family of San Francisco claim knowledge apparently inherited from Thompson's first mate, and Frank Nolan, an Edinburgh telephone engineer, believes that he has derived new information from Thompson's descendants, now in Scotland). Ideally, our authorities to be sought and correlated should be as nearly contemporaneous as possible. The full account of Boucaud's search is contained in *Da Liegt Gold*, by J. Piekalkiewicz. The extremely involved story of the Forbes family and a good deal else, including the confusing role of the controversial Bergmans, are contained in R. Hancock and J. A. Weston's '*The Lost Treasure of Cocos Island*', which is strongly recommended. Most material, it must be said, is rather scattered.

The most promising site is the one in the Bay of Hope. Firstly and pragmatically, it will be looked upon more favourably by the Costa Rican government as a search area, for, worried about effects of expeditions on the ecology of the island (which is a National Park) they would prefer searches to be confined to the coast and to be based from a boat anchored offshore. It will also provide a less exhausting site than the inhospitable terrain inland. Above all however, the experiences of Tony Mangel and Peter Bermans show that there is undoubtedly treasure in this area some of which has been found by design rather than by accident.

Furthermore, if we study the present day chart, at least two of the instructions for finding the *Mary Dear* hoard indicate or seem to indicate this area. The first, written by Thompson himself, instructs the treasure hunter to land at the Bay of Hope in 5 fathoms of water (where a depth of 10m is indicated on the chart), to proceed up the stream for 350 paces and then to head NNE for 850 yards. His clues as to the setting sun, which 'draws silhouette of an eagle with wings spread' are only likely to be understood on the spot. Whatever the arrangement of shadows thrown by the sun setting NW of Mt Iglesias (which it does in the winter) and carefully placed stakes, one thing is certain: the instructions lead us to a point about 1.5 km inland from the north side of the Bay of Hope, due north of three points shown on the chart. These points tie in very well with Keating's own notes which begin 'At two cables lengths, south of the last watering-place, on three points. The cave is the one which is to be found under the second point.' Two cable lengths is 405 yards, and at exactly this distance south of the last of three streams which fall over the cliffs into the sea, we find the second of three points. Keating's notes also say, 'A path must be opened up to the cave from the west.' At low water the beach ends at the southernmost point.

FAST CASTLE, EYEMOUTH, BORDERS, SCOTLAND
THE ARMADA INVASION FUNDS

As the Armada sailed north towards Britain in 1588, Colonel Sempill, King Philip of Spain's special secret agent in Scotland, travelled to the coast from Edinburgh, took a boat to the mouth of the Forth and kept a rendezvous with a Spanish pinnace lying there. On his return he was arrested and specifically searched for incriminating documents or Spanish coin. Nothing was found, but Sempill was thought then, and is still thought today, to be the likeliest candidate for the rôle of Spanish paymaster in Scotland.

The Spanish strategy relied very heavily on popular discontent in Britain, particularly amongst the persecuted but still powerful recusant Catholics. Without support, the Spanish and the Duke of Parma's forces might win to London but could never sustain control. It is for this reason that the wrecked Armada warships sunk off the British and Irish coast have proved such a rich source of treasure. If their initiative was to prove successful, the Spaniards needed a great deal of money to appease the British and to ease their way.

When 'God blew with his wind and they were scattered', ships' captains headed for the Catholic centres of Scotland and Ireland, where they hoped they might be welcomed. The wind, however, kept blowing, and some forty vessels were lost. One ship commanded by Admiral Gomez de Medina, the only survivor of twenty sunk near Fair Isle, limped to shore at Anstruther on the east coast of Scotland.

Twenty miles to the north of Berwick-upon-Tweed, on the eastern coast of Scotland, the ruins of an ancient castle perch on a rugged and lonely crag. Fast Castle has been in ruins for centuries now, but in other days it was a formidable stronghold.

Robert Logan of Restalrig

Six years after the Armada, Robert Logan of Restalrig, master of Fast Castle, developed an obsessive interest in lost treasure. Logan was a wealthy landowner. One of his estates stretched east of Holyrood House in Edinburgh to the coastal port of Leith and included Holyrood Park. He also owned a mill at Anstruther, not far up the coast from Fast.

In July 1594, in a document still preserved amongst the papers of the Napier family, Logan made an extraordinary deal with John Napier of Merchistoun. Napier, an extremely gifted man, is primarily famous for his work in the field of logarithms. He was also renowned in his time as a magician. His high tower south of Edinburgh was known as the Astrologer's Tower.

The subject of the agreement was the proposed search for a treasure hidden somewhere within Fast Castle. If it was found, Napier was to receive one third, an indication of the high value which Logan set on Napier's 'Craft' and 'ingyne', mentioned in the document. The document is recorded in an early inventory as 'a contract of magic', which may furnish some idea of Logan's expectations in that superstitious time. Dowsing is also known to have been one of Napier's many skills.

It seems fairly certain that they failed in their enterprise. One amusing proof of the rancour occasioned by this failure survives in a lease dated 1596. Napier, in letting out land to a tenant, stipulates in the terms of the agreement that

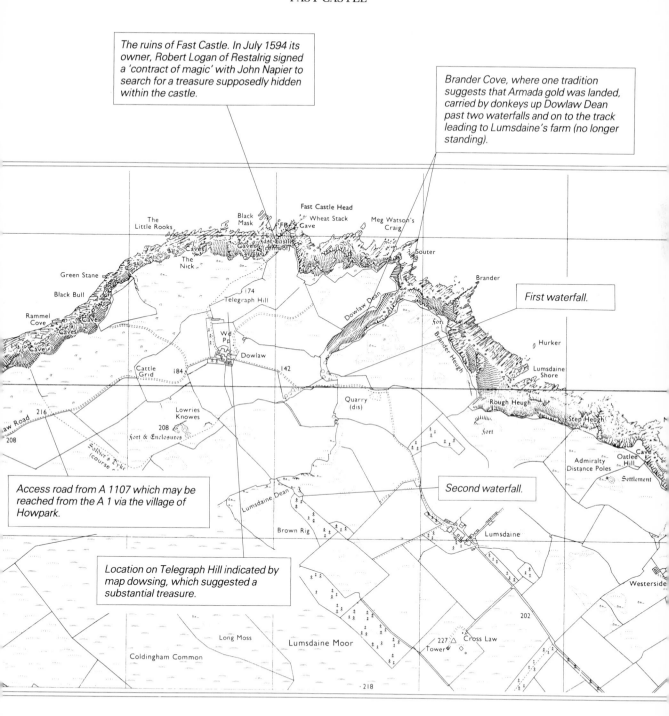

The ruins of Fast Castle. In July 1594 its owner, Robert Logan of Restalrig signed a 'contract of magic' with John Napier to search for a treasure supposedly hidden within the castle.

Brander Cove, where one tradition suggests that Armada gold was landed, carried by donkeys up Dowlaw Dean past two waterfalls and on to the track leading to Lumsdaine's farm (no longer standing).

First waterfall.

Access road from A 1107 which may be reached from the A 1 via the village of Howpark.

Second waterfall.

Location on Telegraph Hill indicated by map dowsing, which suggested a substantial treasure.

Map of the coast of south-east Scotland around Fast Castle, approximately 20 miles north of Berwick-upon-Tweed, reproduced from the Ordnance Survey Map (Sheet NT 86/96). Crown Copyright reserved. Scale 1:25,000.

under no circumstance may the tenant ever sublet his land to anyone by the name of Logan!

This does not seem to have been the first occasion on which Logan tried to make such a deal. There is evidence that in 1593 he had struck a similar bargain with the Earl of Bothwell, another man believed by contemporaries to have magical powers. The King's Privy Council later denounced Logan for his secret dealings with Bothwell, and Logan is on record as having admitted that Bothwell stayed with him.

At the beginning of the seventeenth century, Logan made yet another bargain, this time with Lord Gowrie. They would conduct a joint search of the castle for treasure. Gowrie was to receive the lion's share of any wealth discovered, while Logan would take in exchange Gowrie's castle of Dirleton near North Berwick. The search was to be conducted, it seems, with the utmost secrecy and circumspection.

The story now takes an extraordinary turn. On the eve of Gowrie's planned trip to Fast, his elder brother, the Master of Ruthven, apprehended a strange man in the grounds of his house in Perth, 'a base-like fellow', it was recorded, 'unknown to him, with a cloak cast about his mouth'. When Ruthven seized this man, he found under his arm, 'a great wide pot, all full of coined gold in great pieces'. The coins were said to have been of foreign mintage. Ruthven placed the stranger in custody and at once rode off to find the King, James VI, later King James I of England.

James VI of Scotland, later to become James I of England. In 1600, the King was invited to the house of Lord Ruthven in Perth and his men, fearing an attempt to assassinate the King, killed Ruthven and his brother Gowrie. The treasure of Fast Castle may be at the heart of this tragic tale.

The Gowrie Conspiracy

The king was to relate this story on the following day, after Ruthven and his brother were both dead. The events of this extraordinary night are commonly referred to as the Gowrie Conspiracy, for it was widely believed that the brothers had lured James to their house with a tale of treasure, intending to kidnap or assassinate him there. The Gowries had twice plotted to kidnap the king before.

In conjunction with our knowledge of Gowrie's contract with Logan, however, and the extraordinary coincidence whereby the king is summoned to see treasure at one place just as Gowrie leaves in search of another, it is possible to sketch a different hypothesis.

When Ruthven rode to the king, presumably with some sort of deal in mind, Gowrie knew nothing of the arrest of the stranger or of the gold coins that he carried. Whether Ruthven knew of his brother's deal with Logan is not known. It is reasonable to suppose, however, in the light of this coincidence, that the stranger was an emissary from Logan, come to Perth to see Gowrie and, perhaps, to offer evidence of the presence of Spanish gold at Fast.

Ruthven captured this man, saw the gold and at

once came to certain conclusions. Either he had extracted the true story of the Fast Castle treasure and sought to use the knowledge for his own ends in a trade with the king, or he believed his brother to be involved in some treason and intended to expose him, or quite simply, he thought to win favour with James by delivering to him a hoard of foreign gold. Either way, he was interfering with Gowrie's plans. It must be remembered that Gowrie had staked a great castle against the gold to be found at Fast. He therefore believed the hoard to be very considerable.

When, therefore, Ruthven returned with the king and Gowrie became aware that all his dreams of wealth were about to be shattered, it may have been he who drew his dirk to prevent the revelation of his as yet undiscovered source of wealth. However the fight started, someone drew, and the king's men, presumably forewarned by a justifiably apprehensive king of the risk of an assassination attempt, fell on both Gowries and ran them through.

The stranger vanished. Logan, chastened and presumably afraid after such an event, fell silent. No more is heard of searches for gold at Fast.

Evidence of Witchcraft

Interest in the story was not reawakened until 1969, when investigations of the castle site were made on sea and land. The principal discoveries were found buried in the floor of the back court—

Fast Castle, a ruin on a lonely clifftop in the Scottish border country, may hold the secret of Spanish gold brought ashore in the wake of the Armada. As early as 1594 its owner, Robert Logan, was attempting to locate a hoard. This photograph shows a recent exploration of the site.

some few coins of Elizabeth I and James I, a 38 lb cannonball, a curious collection of animal bones, human leg bones and a skull. Some locals maintain that the skull constitutes evidence of witchcraft.

Another school of thought, unrelated to the Gowrie Conspiracy, maintains that the treasure which Logan sought was not Spanish gold but the silver casket and casket letters of Mary, Queen of Scots, which are known to have been in the possession of an earlier Lord Gowrie in 1584. When this Lord Gowrie was executed for conspiracy soon afterwards, the occupants of Fast Castle were served with a six-hour notice to vacate the premises, probably in order that a search should be made. These letters were eagerly sought in the 1580s. Elizabeth I offered rewards for them and Mary Queen of Scots vowed vengeance on anyone who should surrender them unless to the Crown. Their content is believed to be such as might bring James I's right of succession into question. The overwhelming likelihood, however, in the light of the Gowrie Conspiracy is that Logan believed a large cache of Spanish gold to lie in or near Fast Castle and had found some part of it.

FURTHER ACTION

There are various traditions relating to Fast Castle which may reward further investigation. It is thought, for example, that an old staircase is lost somewhere in the castle. Mr Lumsdaine of Wales, whose family lived on neighbouring land, maintains that the gold was brought in at Brander Cove, a mile or two south-east of Fast, and carried by donkeys up the course of the Dowlaw Burn, past two waterfalls and on to a cart track leading to the Lumsdaines' farm (which is no longer standing). There are several smugglers' hiding places along the coast. No intensive investigation of Fast and area has yet been undertaken.

Documentary evidence may give some indication as to whether the incumbent of Fast at the time of the Armada would have concealed the treasure in the castle or whether David Graham of Fintry, the underground leader thought by some to have concealed the Spanish loot, would have been forced to consider a spot nearby. There cannot have been much time for digging or complicated engineering, and every indication is that the treasure is of gold or silver.

GUADALUPE DE TAYOPA, SONORA, MEXICO
LOST JESUIT SILVER MINES

Four bells, the largest weighing 28 arrobas and 17 pounds [a total of 727 pounds] on which were inscribed TAYOPA. One bell inscribed REMEDIOS. Weight 11 arrobas and 10 pounds.

One small bell inscribed PIEDAD. Weight 5 arrobas. These bells were cast in 1603 by the Right Reverend Father Ignacio Maria de Retana.

One high cross of carved silver from the Tayopa mine, weight 1 arroba, 15 pounds, with an attached crucifix of hammered gold from the Paramo placer.

A pair of processional candle holders and six bars of hammered silver, weighing 4 arrobas, 13 pounds from Santo Niño Mine.

Four incensories of silver and gold plated, weighing 1 arroba, 3 pounds from the Cristo Mine.

In a cut-stone box are stored jewellery. Box is buried in basement under room built of stone and mud, between the church and side of convent and fruit garden.

One large custody with silver bracket, weighing 1 arroba from Santo Niño Mine, with gold glimmer from placer El Paramo and four fine mounted stones from Remedios Mine.

Two silver chalices from the Jesus Maria y Jose Mine, and twelve solid gold cups.

Six gold plates made from Cristo Mine and Purisima Mine, and two large communion plates of gold made from placer El Paramo.

One shrine with four hammered silver columns weighing 4 arrobas from Señor de la Buena Muerto Mine.

Sixty-five cargas [packloads] of silver packed in cow-hide bags, each containing 8 arrobas, 12 pounds.

Eleven cargas of gold from four mines and placer El Paramo, each wrapped in cloth and cow-hide, with a total weight of 99 arrobas [2512 pounds].

Also 183 arrobas of Castilla ore, and 65 arrobas first-class Castilla ore from El Paramo, with a known assay of 22 carats, clean and without mercury.

For the knowledge of our Vicar General, I have written this to inform our Superior.

This inventory, written by a Jesuit and sealed on 17 February, 1646, was found by Henry O. Flipper, the Spanish legal expert, surveyor and historian of mines and mining, in 1911. It tallies almost exactly with another of the same date which had been in the possession of the priest of Guadalupe de Santa Ana, a tiny village in Sonora, Mexico, and which came to light in 1927. Both are headed:

A true and positive description of the mining camp Real of Our Lady of Guadalupe of Tayopa, made in January 1646, by the Right Reverend Father Guardian Fray, Francisco Villegas Garsina y Orosco, Royal Vicar-General of the Royal and Distinguished Jesuit Order of Saint Ignacio of Tayopa, and Jesuit of the Great Faculty of the Province of Sonora and Biscalla, whom may God keep long years.

Both list the number of mines at or around Guadalupe de Tayopa as seventeen.

For many years before these documents were found, there had been tales of a *real de minas*—a group of mines—at a place known only as Tayopa. This was the first time that its full name had been discovered.

Now it only remained, it seemed, to identify Guadalupe de Tayopa and to search for the treasure in the church vaults and for the mines in the mountains.

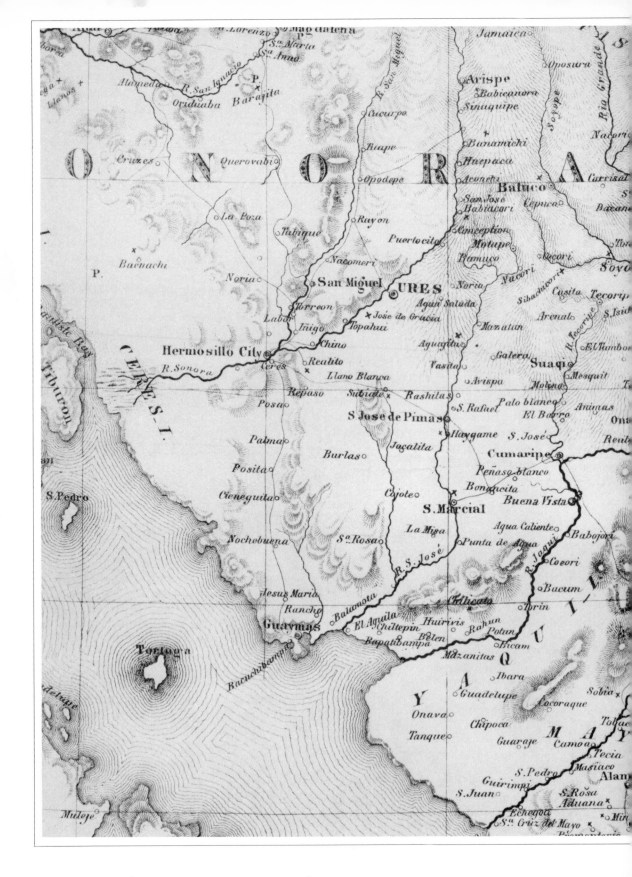

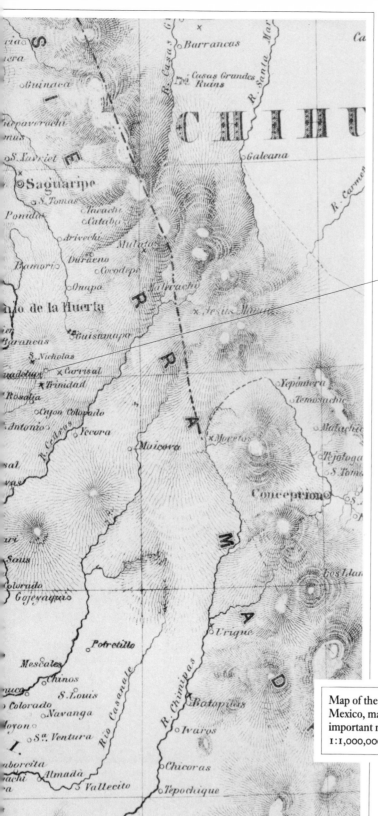

Neither Guadalupe de Tayopa nor Guadalupe de Santa Ana appear on modern maps, but this mid-nineteenth-century mining map shows a village named 'Guadelupe' in a location where a village of this name has not since been identified and very close to where Tayopa or Santa Ana were thought to be.

Map of the Gadsden Purchase showing part of Sonora, Mexico, made in Cincinnati in 1858. The crosses indicate important mining districts. Scale approximately 1:1,000,000.

Henry O. Flipper, the first black graduate of West Point military academy, was Tayopa's most ardent seeker, even travelling to Spain for further clues.

The Jesuit Mines

It may at first sight seem odd that a *real de minas* of such legendary richness should simply have disappeared from written history and from the face of the map. It must be remembered, however, that, although many of Mexico's mines were owned by Jesuits, it was illegal under Spanish law for priests to own and operate mines. This law was initially passed in 1592 and reiterated in 1621 in the face of gross violation by the Jesuits. In 1703, a royal decree was passed to reprove those who were consistently breaking this law.

It was in the interests of the Jesuits, therefore, to keep their mines secret—not least because they would have wished, as at Plazuela, to avoid having to pay the Royal Fifth to their king.

The first Mexican finds seem to have been made in 1600 when a rich lode of silver was discovered in Chihuahua. Sometime around 1603, according to our inventory, the mines now known collectively as Tayopa were discovered in Sonora, the westernmost province of northern Mexico, which rapidly became famous as one of the richest mining regions in the world. Zacatecas, Aguascalientes, San Luis Potosi, Guanajuato, San Miguel de Allende and Queretaro, now architectural gems on the tourist circuit, were once mining towns that owed their existence and in due course their pomp and magnificence to mineral wealth. Even today, the town of Pachuca has the largest output of silver in the world.

In *Frutos En Que Comercia O Puede Comerciar la Nueva Espana* (*Fruits In Which New Spain Trades*) by Father Francisco Javier Clavijero, published in 1767, we find the following reference to '*Projecto Sobre La Sonora*' ('The Sonora Project'): 'La Sonora ... is the province that is the richest in gold and silver. What is said of it in the History of California is no exaggeration; that "there are mountains there that are of little less than solid silver".'

Father Clavijero also described, however, the principal hazard of the area:

These mines were first worked by various individuals, but when the Royal Council of the Indies declared that they were not mines, but treasure trove, and as such belonged to the Royal patrimony, the workers withdrew, and they were abandoned to the incursions of the barbarians. These incursions which prevent the working of extremely rich mines, which there are in the provinces of Primeria, Sonora, Tarahumana, Tepehuana and others of New Vizcaya could be avoided by the erection of various strongholds and fortresses along the frontiers with the Apaches—according to representations made to the Viceroys by various zealous missionaries of the Company [i.e. the Jesuits].

One of the first detailed maps of Mexico and California, made by the Jesuit, Father Kino, in 1701. The map does not indicate Tayopa, which may already have been deserted by that date. The River Yaqui is marked on the map as Hiakin and, to the south, on the River Mayo (Majo) we see the only Guadalupe.

TABULA CALIFORNIÆ Anno 1702.
Ex autoptica observatione delineata à R.P. Chino e S.I.
Via terrestris in Californiam comperta et detecta Per R. Patrem Eusebium Fran. Chino e S.I. Germanum. Adnotatis novis Missionibus eiusdem Soc.tis ab Anno 1698. ad annum 1701.
Milliaria Gallica
Ingentes Montes ad Hilam usque protensi
Moqui
NOVUM MEXICUM
Apaches
Alchedomas
Coloratus fl. seu Nord = Strom
Cutganes 1701.
S. Dionysius 1700.
Hoabonomas
YUMAS
Cocomaricopas
Bagiopas
Sobaipotis
Pimeria
Casa Grande
Blaubero
Quiquimas.
Schneeberg
CALIFORNIÆ
MARE CALIFORNIÆ
SONORA
Topokis
Guaimas
Hiakin
Portus S. Sabina
2. Saltz-Insel
Wall-Fisch Seichte
B. de Balenas
B. de Sablas oder Sand-Seichte
Portus Novi Anni inventus. 1685.
MARE DEL ZUR oder SUD = MEER
Loreto
Edues
Yodivinege
Baya S. Lucæ
CINALOA
NOVA GALLICIA
Chalaca
Tropicus Canceri
PARS
Prom. S. Lucæ
Annotatio.
Pars hujus Tabulæ A.B.C.D. è Chartâ Topographicâ R.P. Eusebi Francisci Chino fuit tran

Guadalupe de Tayopa

Some traditions maintain that Tayopa was razed after only fourteen years in the great Apache uprising of 1646, thus dating its foundation to 1632; however it is clear from Father Clavijero's account more than a hundred years later that the Jesuits maintained an active interest in the area.

Other evidence shows that Tayopa was inhabited regularly or even continuously during the late seventeenth and early eighteenth centuries. Flipper, the most dedicated and successful of Tayopa seekers, found documents referring to marriages and deaths in Tayopa in a village in Eastern Sonora. Other Tayopa records were discovered in the town of Granados. In 1927, Carl Sauer of the University of California, trapped by rain in Arizpe, Sonora, inspected a chest full of documents including marriage banns drawn up at Tayopa shortly before 1700. Various 'miners of Tayopa' testified in these as to the pure Spanish blood of the men and women to be married. Sauer also learned that the baptismal records of Tayopa were kept at Bacadeguachi. 'The records that I saw established the fact that, in the seventeenth century, Tayopa was a mining camp of sufficient importance to have its own *cura* (priest). At that time there were probably not three other *curas* in what is now the state of Sonora. If it had a *cura*, it had a church. The church should have been built of stone; if so, remains of it should be evident today. The Apaches were very hostile towards the close of the seventeenth century; my guess is that Tayopa had to be abandoned because of them. I judge it lay somewhere between Nacori Chico and Guaynopa.'

Britton Davies, an officer in the United States army, was leading troops in pursuit of Apaches in 1885 when he came to Nacori. He found there, he says, 'a curious state of affairs. The population was three hundred and thirteen souls; but of these only fifteen were adult males. Every family had lost one or more male members at the hands of the Apaches.'

He also heard here of the lost mines of Tayopa. 'This mine was said to have been of such wonderful richness that blocks of silver taken from it had to be cut into several pieces so that mules could carry them to the sea coast for shipment to Spain. My informant, the white-haired *presidente*, a man over eighty years of age, told me that his grandfather, who also had lived to be a very old man, had worked in the mine as a boy, and that it was in a mountain range to the east of Nacori.

'The Apaches attacked the place one day when the men were nearly all away at a *fiesta* in one of the river (Rio Bavispe) towns, killed everyone in the camp, destroyed the buildings, and blew up the entrance to the mine. A hundred years went by with no force in the country strong enough to conquer the Apaches, and the mine has never been found.'

The *presidente*'s grandfather had also stated that 'Here in Nacori, where we stand, on a still night one could hear the dogs bark and the church bells ring in Tayopa.' If we take the *presidente*'s evidence literally and assume that the word 'grandfather' was not, as in many tongues, a generic word for an ancestor, it is unlikely, although not impossible, that his grandfather could have been working at the mine earlier than, say, 1720.

The Gold and Silver Bell

Whether as a result of the Jesuit expulsion order in 1767, or as a result of Apache depredations, then, the mines at Tayopa seem to have been

Carl Sauer, a Californian scholar, learned during the course of his researches that the baptismal records of Guadalupe de Tayopa were stored in the church of the town of Bacadeguachi.

A Jesuit missionary preaching. The presence of missionaries proved a mixed blessing for the Indians. While acquiring skills, artefacts and a new religion, the Indians too often sacrificed their independence, and many were driven into total slavery.

'Throughout history and throughout the world,' says Alan Hughes of the Whitechapel Bell foundries, 'Bells have been cast in bell metal, an alloy of copper and tin, because their brittleness gives the bell its tone. Soft metals are totally impracticable.' If, therefore, this bell existed, it was not a church bell, but might, perhaps, have been a memento cast by the mines, or even a Jesuit device to disguise a large amount of precious

Captain James Hobbs, who himself lived amongst the Indians for a time, was one of a party of bounty-hunters who pursued a band of Apaches to the headwaters of the Yaqui River in 1842. After a successful attack on an Indian village, they found the 'ancient ruins' of a large mining settlement which may well have been Tayopa.

closed and the village itself lost by the mid-eighteenth century. Flipper, incidentally, heard of another tradition that, from Tayopa, one could hear the dogs barking in Guaynopa. This proximity of the two settlements may find confirmation in the evidence of a bell of gold and silver which was dug up near the Sonoran border in 1896, but has since been melted down. The legend inscribed upon it read, 'TAYOPA, GUAYNO-PA, GUAYNOPITA, SONORA. TRES MINERALES DEL MUNDO'. This has been mistranslated as 'the three mines of the world' and even, by optimistic implication, 'the three richest mines of the world'. We can find no evidence, however, that the word 'minerale' has ever been used to mean 'mine'. The legend, simply translated, means 'three minerals of the world'—a reference, perhaps, to gold, silver and copper.

metal. It is, at any rate, an unsatisfactory piece of evidence.

James Kirker's Discovery

In 1842, James Kirker, riding with a party of seventy Shawnee warriors, came to a ruined town on the western slopes of the Sierra Madre, which many have since believed to have been Tayopa. Kirker was a bounty-hunter, who made his living by collecting Apache scalps. He was pursuing a large band of Apaches who had captured some freight near Vera Cruz and killed many Mexicans.

'In wonderfully rich country,' beside a lake some six to eight miles across, wrote Captain James Hobbs, who was riding with Kirker, 'we found some ancient ruins, the cement walls and foundation stones of a church and a *lignum vitae* cross, which seemed as sound as it had ever been. We also found remains of a smelting furnace ... and some drops of silver and copper. From the appearance of the ruins, it seemed as if there had been a considerable town there. The lake was the headwaters of the river Yaqui ... Besides the remains of furnaces, we saw old mine shafts that had been worked, apparently long before. Specimens of gold, silver and copper ore that we took to the mint at Chihuahua were assayed and pronounced very rich.'

Whether this was Tayopa—and it may well have been—it is not likely to be the same site as that seen by Casimero Streeter just a few years later. Streeter was a 'white Apache', a renegade white man who lived and fought for some years with the Indians. He was on a raiding-party to the south-east of Cananea in Northern Sonora, when his fellow braves pointed to some ruins way below in a canyon and told him, 'That is Tayopa, leave it alone. Never try to go to it.' He could just make out a bell in the ruined church tower. He subsequently identified this spot as lying on a fork of the River Yaqui. Neither the canyon nor the church bell are mentioned in Hobbs's account of the town which he visited. It is therefore unlikely that they are the same, though both are said to be on the Yaqui, from whose headwaters, Hobbs tells us, 'the Indians [i.e. Mayos] bring down much gold, though they dare not venture far into the mountains for fear of the Apaches.'

The Search for Tayopa

In 1909, Henry O. Flipper, still searching for Tayopa, was living in Ocampo, when a surprising activity was noted in the area: 'Many Jesuits came into the Sierra Madre, taking charge of churches that had for generations been abandoned and even establishing themselves where there were no churches. In one little Indian village without a church there were four Jesuit priests. The mountain natives thought these Jesuits were after Tayopa and other lost mines or hidden treasures. Whatever they were after, the Revolution of 1910 prevented their accomplishing anything.'

In 1910 another attempt to find Tayopa was made by a mining company on the basis of a map copied some fifty years previously by the caretaker of an ancient but regrettably unnamed church in which many Tayopa documents had been housed. This map gave clear directions to Tayopa. Following these, a party of thirty arrived at a remote and hidden valley in Yaqui country. They found traces of adobe houses and between fifteen and twenty mineshafts some eighty feet deep and full of water. The samples of ore which they took there proved rich in silver. They returned to civilization, founded a new company named Cinco de Mayo, staked their claim to the site, and were poised to sell out to some larger company which could exploit the mines properly when the Revolution also put paid to their hopes. The number of mines that they found is consistent with that in the Tayopa inventory, but we have no idea where the site lies.

In 1911, Flipper was in Spain where he discovered a paper giving directions to Tayopa. He quotes it verbatim:

On the 7th day of March stand on the summit of Cerro de la Campana, near the Villa de la Concepcion, and look at the sun as it sets. It will be setting directly over Tayopa. Travel eight days from the Cerro de la Campana towards the sunset of March 7th and you will come to Tayopa.

He was able to identify Cerro de la Campana with considerable confidence as Cerro de la Miñaca, a bell-shaped hill a few miles south of the town now called Guerrero, in Chihuahua. But Flipper could never avail himself of this clue: the Revolution prevented further work in Mexico, and he was sent to Venezuela. He never came back.

In 1927, C. B. Ruggles, a latterday frontiersman and veteran Tayopa hunter, and the writer, J. Frank Dobie were approached at their camp in La Quiparita, a valley to the west of Chihuahua, by a man who gave his name as Custard. Custard possessed an extended version of the original inventory which included directions to Tayopa from a flat-topped mountain or *mesa* named Mesa Campanero. He also had an approximate and highly stylized map which placed Tayopa amidst the hills of the Sierra Madre. These documents had been copied from originals left by Father Domingo, the parish priest of Guadalupe de Santa Ana, a man who was described by an old Indian parishioner as 'a queer man ... always walking about and looking, looking.' Custard proposed that they pool their skills and resources. If they should find the lost village, Custard would take the treasure in the church crypt and Ruggles and Dobie could have the mine.

Ruggles agreed. He believed the Mesa Campanero to be an alternative name for the Sierra Obscura, a mountain which stands alongside the River Mayo.

The three men spent ten days exploring the Sierra, searching for the two *cerritos chapos* or 'runt' hills which were said to form the gateway to Tayopa and the 'two notably thick guerigo trees' mentioned in Custard's directions. They found nothing.

Custard's *derrotero*, a highly stylized guide to Tayopa, was originally derived from one owned by the parish priest of Guadalupe de Santa Ana. Despite this map and a detailed accompanying text, Ruggles's expedition still did not have enough information to lead them to their goal.

Conocimento de Tayopa

On their gloomy descent from the mountain, they stopped at the little range of an Opata rancher named Perfecto Garcia. Garcia's brother had that day pursued a big boar. At bay, it had gored his dog and, when he attacked it with his machete it had turned and nearly slashed off his ear. Ruggles had some skill in medicine. He washed, stitched and bandaged the man's wounds. When he had finished, in Dobie's words, 'Don Perfecto was in an expansive humour.

"Are you not hunting for mines?" he asked Ruggles.

"Yes."

"Do you have any documents to direct you?"

"Yes."

"I have one also. Let me show it to you."'

And incredibly, Garcia drew from a niche in the wall an old parchment entitled 'Conocimento de Tayopa' or 'Recognition of Tayopa'. Ruggles and Dobie copied it eagerly. Garcia informed them that the Opatas had taken the document in a raid on a ranch owned by the Pima Indians. It read, 'It is worthwhile to remember and never to forget that there is a famous mining camp of prodigious richness known to the ancients by the name of Tayopa. It is situated on the first flowings of the River Yaqui, on the downward slopes of the Sierra Madre, in the direction of the town of Yecora in the ancient province of Ostimuri. The smelters remain there not only with great deposits of ore of high assay but with considerable silver in bullion form, stored away just as the *antiguos* left it. During long years Ostimuri has been almost altogether depopulated.' From this point onward, the partly torn parchment was unreadable except for a few disconnected words.

The searchers left immediately for Yecora, which still bore the same name. The natives had seen no strangers for two years and in their own curiosity were happy to answer Ruggles' questions. Asked for directions to Mesa Campanero, they at once pointed to the pine-clad ridge to the west of their village.

Here, on top of the mountain, the party found the 'first flowings of the river Yacqui' to their west. They followed Custard's map from this point. They had already concluded that Guadalupe de Tayopa might be Guadalupe de Santa Ana, but resolved for fear of error to follow the map implicitly. It took them two weeks. Amongst others whom they met were the descendants of some Confederate soldiers who, in the aftermath of the Civil War, had turned their backs on their country. At last they found two giant trees of a variety unfamiliar to them. Ruggles rode ahead to Santa Ana and brought back with him an old man who at once identified them as *guerigos*, which Dobie later ascertained to be *populus wislizeni*.

The Villagers show them the Mines

They followed their road down to the village, passing between two 'runt' hills. After initial hostility from the villagers Ruggles' medical skills once more saved the day. He treated some fifty influenza sufferers over the next three days. Only then did they broach the subject which had brought them so far. Was Guadalupe de Santa Ana really Guadalupe de Tayopa?

To their delight, the villagers, now deep in their debt, showed them the ancient circle of mines. Even the names mentioned on the map and in the inventory were still in current use. The smelters were still there too, and many tools of evidently Spanish provenance.

The villagers told stories of other treasure-seekers who had come to the village and had dug towards the church. It seems probable, however, that the present church, built by Father Domingo in 1888, was not on the same site as that which the Jesuits had built. Flipper at some stage in his researches had come upon a traditional document which claimed that a huge quantity of bullion was secured in a tunnel or vault 2,281 *varas* (about 2,024 yards) east and 63 *varas* (about 57 yards) south of the church door. This tunnel was said to have a metal door or lock. Flipper had been sceptical of this story, but the head of the village independently confirmed it. His mother and aunt, he said, had found an iron door in the ground somewhere east of the village about fifty years before. They had never been able to guide the villagers back to it, and had been subjected to much mockery. Their story had never changed, however, and the village head knew that it must be true.

The villagers gave Ruggles and his party several old *derroteros*, one of which had guided an ill-fated expedition to Tayopa in 1858. A Jesuit had led the party. Only one member had survived. Those who were not killed by Indians on their way, died one way or another at their destination. The sole survivor had been hidden by an Indian girl who later married him.

Ruggles and his party surveyed the mines and made estimates as to the time and money necessary to re-open them. They then, tantalizingly and mysteriously, disappear apart from Dobie who later wrote up the story of their expedition in detail. Dobie suggested that Ruggles returned to Guadalupe de Santa Ana shortly afterwards but does not record that he succeeded in extracting any of the silver ore or in finding the great Jesuit hoard.

FURTHER ACTION

The first essential step of any future search for the

Tayopa treasure must be to find out what happened to Ruggles on his return trip. It is very strange for the narrator of such an account to stop short in the way that Dobie has done with this story and it suggests that either he lost contact with Ruggles or that Ruggles found nothing substantial on his return to the area.

On the *derrotero* in Custard's possession there is an area marked '*Placeres de Paramos*'. A 'placer' is a deposit of sand or gravel in, for example, the bed of a stream which contains particles of valuable minerals. This too might repay investigation.

This is obviously a location where a treasure hunter should take full advantage of the latest developments in electronic prospecting. The vast range of different types and makes of detector on the market may seem bewildering but there are a number of informative books that will guide you through the maze of ore identification, proper detector settings, bench testing of samples, recovery methods, identification of concentrated iron deposits and 'hot rocks', nugget hunting, vein tracing and silver finding as well as helping you to choose the right detector and searchcoil. *Electronic Prospecting* by Charles Garrett, Bob Grant and Roy Lagal is to be recommended.

LUNDY ISLAND, BRISTOL CHANNEL, ENGLAND
NUTT'S PLUNDER CAVE

Lundy is a natural island fortress. A chunk of granite just three miles long and one mile wide, clearly visible from the North Cornwall and Devon coast when rain threatens, though at other times often blanketed in mist, its cliffs are steep and its coves studded with jagged rocks. The Atlantic which surrounds it is savage and treacherous. No coastline in Europe has seen more wrecks and claimed more lives. Lundy has taken a sizeable share of them.

Named after the puffins which, with the other auks and divers literally cover the cliffs to this day, Lundy would be uninhabitable were it not for one landing place at its southernmost end. Very early in history it became a refuge for pirates, outlaws, wreckers and smugglers. In 1238, William de Marisco made the island his base. His son Jordan, also a pirate, succeeded him and held it in defiance of the king. Marisco Castle, still standing though substantially restored was probably built at this time.

The Dreadful de Mariscos

The history of the de Mariscos is turbulent and confused. One of them was accused of sending an assassin to try to kill Henry III in 1238. The assassin was torn limb from limb by horses and de Marisco himself, after six more years of piracy, was 'executed at the Tower ... with special ignominy, his body suspended in a sack, and when stiff in death, disembowelled, his bowels burnt, and his body divided into quarters'.

Although Lundy was then seized by the King, another de Marisco was soon back at his island citadel. The last of them died in 1327 to be succeeded by still more pirates. That Lundy was

deemed to be almost impregnable is demonstrated by the indictment of Lord Seymour, Edward VI's uncle. One of the charges for which he was tried and later executed was that he had wished to acquire Lundy in order that 'being aided with shipps and conspiring at all evill eventes with pirates he might at all tymes have a sure and saufe refuge'.

John and Robert Nutt

In the 1620s, two piratical brothers, John and Robert Nutt, appear in Lundy's history. Sometimes on the side of law, more generally not, they seem, perhaps through friendship in high places, to have been oddly successful in obtaining pardons for their crimes.

On 3 June 1623, Captain Thomas Best reported to the Naval Commissioners that Captain Nutt, the pirate was off the Devonshire Coast. Nutt had captured many prizes, and Best wanted to be sent after him, but within a few days Nutt submitted and brought his ship into harbour. He had committed many wrongs in the last few weeks, he said, and wanted to know whether he was still thought worthy of the pardon he had been formerly offered. Presumably, he was found worthy: at any rate, shortly afterwards he was back to his old tricks.

In 1632, Robert Nutt, now styling himself 'Admiral', with two or more ships under his command, made Lundy his headquarters. He devoted his time mainly to 'pilfering the small traders', and several ships-of-war were detailed to capture him. In May, he was reported to have made for 'the Flemish islands', and his brother was dispatched from Plymouth to take him a copy

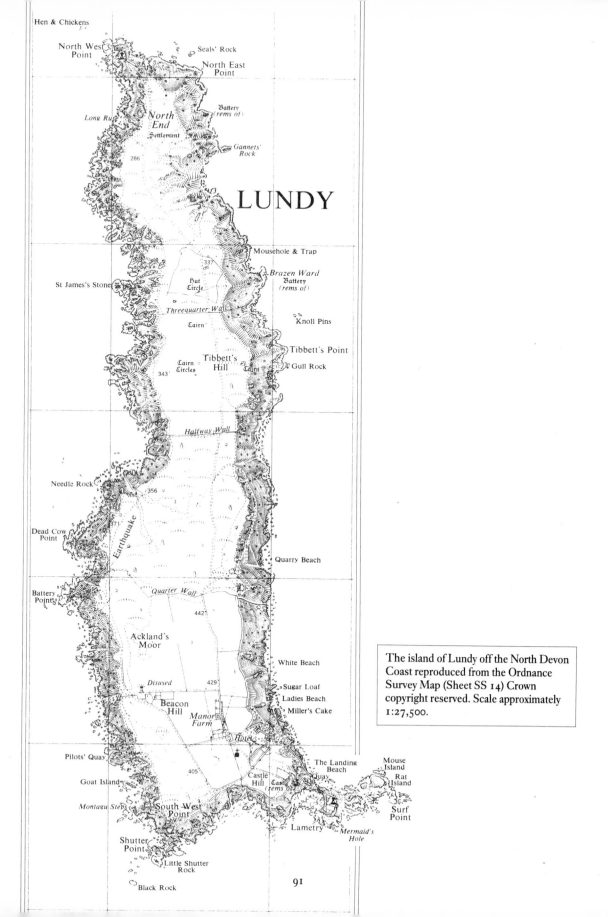

LUNDY

Hen & Chickens
North West Point
Seals' Rock
North East Point
Battery (rems of)
Long Rus
North End
Settlement
Gannets' Rock
286
Mousehole & Trap
337
St James's Stone
Hut Circle
Brazen Ward Battery (rems of)
Threequarter Wall
Cairn
Knoll Pins
Cairn
Tibbett's Point
Cairn Circles
Tibbett's Hill
Cairn
Gull Rock
343
Halfway Wall
Needle Rock
356
Dead Cow Point
371
Earthquake
Quarry Beach
Battery Point
Quarter Wall
442
Ackland's Moor
White Beach
Disused
429
Sugar Loaf
Beacon Hill
Ladies Beach
Miller's Cake
Manor Farm
Hotel
Pilots' Quay
405
The Landing Beach
Mouse Island
Goat Island
Castle Hill
Castle (rems of)
Quay
Rat Island
Montagu Steps
South West Point
Surf Point
Lametry
Mermaid's Hole
Shutter Point
Little Shutter Rock
Black Rock

The island of Lundy off the North Devon Coast reproduced from the Ordnance Survey Map (Sheet SS 14) Crown copyright reserved. Scale approximately 1:27,500.

91

The treacherous west coast of Lundy, where the plunder of the notorious Captain Nutt, who used the island as his base in the 1630s, is said to be hidden. Two men exploring the cave in 1864 died in a rock fall and this has understandably deterred other searchers.

of yet another pardon. 'The opinion of the country is that when the one brother finds out the other he will join with him in that devilish trade,' says a contemporary record.

On 4 September, a Captain Plumleigh caught up with the pirate fleet, 'bestowing upon them thirty great shot, of which Nutt received ten through his own ship, but they succeeded in escaping.'

During Nutt's residence on Lundy, he is supposed to have established a vast cache in one of the island's caves. Returning one day from a raid in the Bristol Channel, he encountered two British men-of-war. His ship, the *Black Mary*, fled towards the Welsh Coast, where it foundered, taking the whole crew with it.

The Cave

After his death, the islanders long remembered where he is said to have stored his loot—in a cave at the foot of a 365 ft. cliff on the dangerous west coast. At high tide, the opening of this cave is, or was, covered by the sea.

The treasure is said to be accursed, and the cave itself haunted. This may explain why the story was not investigated till 1864. In that year, two bold islanders ventured inside with fatal results: a sudden rock fall trapped them, and the sea saw to the rest. Not till over seventy years had passed did anyone even get so far as to finding their skeletons.

FURTHER ACTION

In view of the confusion concerning the two pirates—a recent authority gives the first names of both brothers for the Lundy pirate in separate parts of the same page—the history of these two must be studied closely in contemporary records. A modern Lundy expert, Tony Langham, links Robert Nutt with Ireland and believes it was exclusively John who was associated with Lundy. This opposes older authorities such as the nineteenth-century Chanter. Confirmation of the fate of the *Black Mary* would also be desirable. Rumours were rife about Robert Nutt who, according to one account, was hanged for piracy by the Spaniards.

The cave will not be difficult to find and must be carefully distinguished from Benson's cave on the south side, close to Marisco Castle, another pirate haunt. My authority concerning the cave, suggests there may be considerable danger from the sea, and the tides must be carefully studied.

MONTVALE, BEDFORD COUNTY, VIRGINIA, USA
THE 'BEALE CODES' MINING CACHE

In 1862, Robert Morriss, a worthy and trusted burgher of Lynchburg in the state of Virginia, summoned a young man named James B. Ward to his house. Ward was the son of old family friends whom Morriss 'would benefit if he could'. The old man explained that, as his life drew to an end, he felt constrained to pass on some important information which only he possessed.

At first, he was cautious and hesitant. Ward, though impatient, was careful not to urge him too fast or too far. As the weeks went by, Morriss's hesitancy vanished and he spoke more freely. His story was of the days, some forty years ago, when he had been keeping Lynchburg's principal hotel.

Morriss had entered the hotel trade on his wife's advice, after his tobacco business had failed. By dint of his 'kind disposition, strict probity, excellent management and well-ordered household' he and his hotel became well-known even beyond the state borders. He was not only an amiable host to his paying guests, but a philanthropic one to those who could not pay, sometimes giving them food and shelter for months at a stretch. This approachability and reputation for straight dealing no doubt influenced people to confide in him. The story he now told sprang from one such confidence.

Lynchburg, Virginia, where Thomas Jefferson Beale entrusted some mysterious ciphers to a local hotel-keeper. The partially solved ciphers refer to a fortune in gold, silver and jewels.

Thomas Jefferson Beale

In January 1820, Thomas Jefferson Beale and two friends came to stay at the hotel. Morriss gave a full, if somewhat uncritical description of Beale: 'He was about six feet in height, with jet black eyes and hair of the same color, worn longer than was the style at that time. His form was symmetrical, and gave evidence of unusual strength and activity; but his distinguishing feature was a dark and swarthy complexion, as if much exposure to the sun had thoroughly tanned and discolored him; this however did not detract from his appearance, and I thought him the handsomest man I had ever seen. Altogether, he was a model of manly beauty, favoured by the ladies and envied by men. To the first, he was reverentially tender and polite; to the latter, affable and courteous, but, if they were supercilious or presuming, the lion was aroused, and woe to the man who

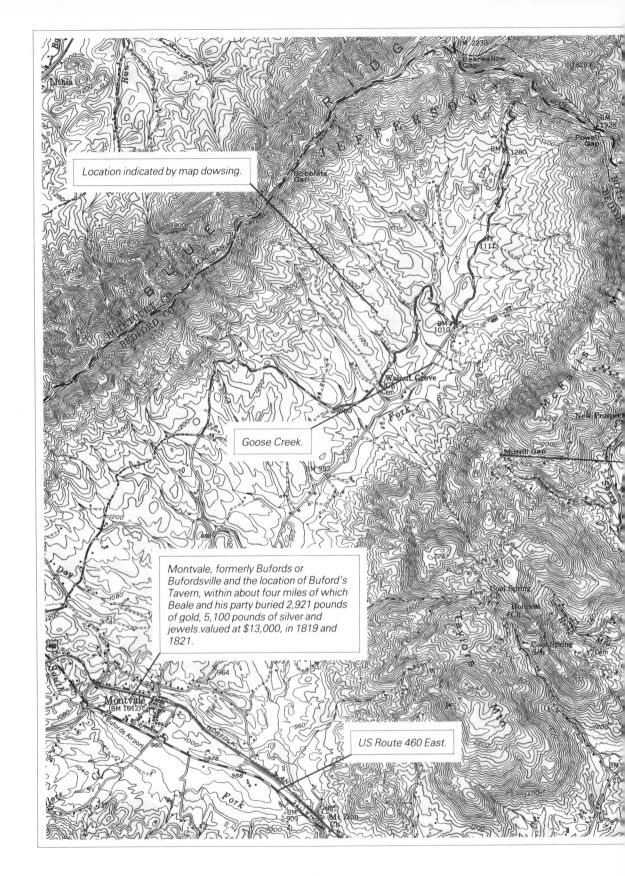

Location indicated by map dowsing.

Goose Creek.

Montvale, formerly Bufords or
Bufordsville and the location of Buford's
Tavern, within about four miles of which
Beale and his party buried 2,921 pounds
of gold, 5,100 pounds of silver and
jewels.valued at $13,000, in 1819 and
1821.

US Route 460 East.

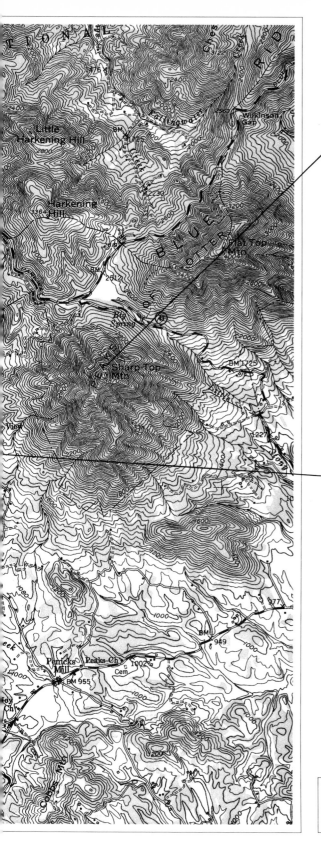

The Peaks of Otter.

In the Beale Papers, Beale referred to a trail 'that bordered Goose Creek' which led through a gap in the Blue Ridge foothills near the Peaks of Otter. Was this Murrill Gap?

Map of Montvale and part of the Blue Ridge Mountains, from the USGS Peaks of Otter Quadrangle, Virginia. Scale 1:50,000.

offended him.'

This paragon signed the register as 'of Virginia', and announced that he would remain at the hotel for the remainder of the winter. His two friends would be leaving in a few days for Richmond, which was close to their homes.

When they had gone Beale established himself as a general favourite. In March, his friends returned to collect him. He was not to come back to Lynchburg for a further two years.

Beale's story is no doubt true that he had come to Lynchburg expressly in order to size up the hotelier and to judge the truth of the excellent reports of him that he had heard. What is clear is that he came to trust Morriss as much as any man living, for, on a second stay between January and March 1822, he left in Morriss's care a locked iron box which, he said, contained papers of great importance. He asked Morriss to look after it until it should be called for. Morriss readily assented, locked the box in the safe and thought no more of it.

Soon afterwards, however, Morriss received an unexpected letter from Beale. It was dated 9 May 1822 and sent from St. Louis where, Beale said, he had arrived just the day before. He was now on the way to the plains, he wrote, to hunt buffalo and to search for grizzlies. He expected to be gone for at least two years.

He stressed the importance of the box. It contained papers, he said, 'vitally affecting the fortunes of myself and many others engaged in business with me, and in the event of my death, its loss might be irreparable'. The papers comprised some letters addressed to Morriss and 'other papers unintelligible without the aid of a key to assist you'. If within ten years, no one had come for the box, Morriss was then to open it. A friend would send him the key in June 1832. Beale also asked that Morriss should appoint someone else to do this if he should somehow be prevented from fulfilling the request himself.

'I have been thus particular in my instructions, in consequence of the somewhat perilous enterprise in which we are engaged, but trust we shall meet long ere the time expires and so save you this trouble. Be the result what it may, however, the game is worth the candle, and we will play it to the end.'

I quote this letter at length largely in order to demonstrate that, although florid in style, the tone is evenly modulated, the grammar correct and the syntax precise. This is neither the letter of a mad nor desperate man. It corresponds with what we know of Beale, who seems in every way to have been stable, intelligent and trustworthy. Nothing more was heard of Beale or from him. He must have died somewhere on the plains.

The Beale Codes

No one had returned for the box or brought Morriss the key by the end of June 1832, but Morriss, scrupulous to a fault, did not think it proper to break the lock until 1845. Inside were two letters and three series of numbers; there were no other papers 'except two or three of an unimportant character, and having no connection with the subject in hand'.

The letters were dated 5 January and 6 January 1822. Both had been written at Lynchburg. The first letter explained the source of the mystery. Beale related that, in 1817, he and thirty friends had set off from Virginia to hunt big game on the Western Plains. They left St. Louis on 19 May and headed for Santa Fe. They intended to be absent for two years. Their guide advised them 'to form a regular military organization, with a captain'. The party elected Beale as that captain.

On 1 December they arrived in Santa Fe, intending to winter there. They grew bored and restless, and 'early in March, some of the party, to vary the monotony of their lives, determined upon a short excursion'. They expected to be back in a few days. After four or five weeks, therefore, with no sign of them, the other members of the party were naturally worried. Beale was about to send out scouts when two of them appeared with a remarkable story.

They had enjoyed good sport, they said, and were on the point of turning back to Santa Fe when they caught sight of a huge herd of buffalo. They pursued the herd for over a fortnight until one night they pitched camp 'in a small ravine, some two hundred and fifty or three hundred miles to the North of Santa Fe'. They were collecting wood and cooking when one of the men ran back to the camp-fire with a lump of rock in

The only part of the Beale Codes to have been deciphered reveals that the treasure lies buried in a vault six feet underground, about four miles from Montvale in Bedford County, Virginia. It is thought to lie to the east, in the Blue Ridge Mountain range, somewhere near the Peaks of Otter.

his hand. A brief consultation confirmed his suspicions. It was gold, and there was a great deal more clearly visible in the rock face. Two messengers were at once dispatched to fetch Beale and the rest of the party.

Beale found a deal of excited activity and little order in the ravine. The men had improvised tools and collected a small heap of ore. Beale organized them and hired some Indian labourers to help. By the end of eighteen months they had accumulated a large quantity of gold and some silver. They could not stay there forever without their secret being known, and the ravine was in the heart of the lawless West. It was decided that the gold should be transported to a cave known to all of them 'near Buford's tavern in the county of Bedford'. They would all set out on the hazardous

journey but, after five hundred miles, only Beale and ten others would go on.

The journey was safely completed, but the cave was no longer the secret place of Beale's youth. He found it in use as a store for local farmers' vegetables. Without much difficulty, however, Beale and his companions selected another site, somewhere in the Blue Ridge Mountains, dug a vault and buried their hoard.

The treasure was to be split thirty ways. Each member of the party was to receive one share. Ever aware, however, of the perils of lives spent in hunting and prospecting in Indian country, each member had named another person who was to inherit the stake in the event of his death. This, Beale's letter revealed, was why he had sought out Morriss. He was to go to the cache and to deliver to each of the named beneficiaries his share. In return, Morriss himself was allocated a thirty-first share 'as you have been unanimously made one of our association, and as such are entitled to share equally with the others'.

After his first departure from Lynchburg in March 1820, Beale had returned to the site to find the work 'still progressing favorably'. He recruited many more Indians and again returned to Virginia in the autumn of 1821 and deposited 'an increased supply of metal' at the same site.

Of the numbered papers, Beale stated: 'they will be unintelligible without the key which will reach you in time and will be found merely to state the contents of our depository, with its exact location, and a list of the names of our party, with their places of residence etc. I thought at first to give you their names in this letter, but reflecting that some one may read the letter, and thus be enabled to impose upon you by personating some member of the party, have decided the present plan is best.'

Beale's second letter appears to have been a superfluous afterthought, to remind Morriss that the paper listing the members of the party and their selected beneficiaries would enable him to distribute the gold justly.

Morriss, of course, could not break the code without the key. When he handed all the papers over to Ward in 1862, he merely made some honourable stipulations as to the distribution of the treasure should it ever be found. Ward was to receive one half of Morriss's share, one sixty-second.

James Ward the Code-Breaker

Ward set to work with great enthusiasm. The following year, Morriss died. At first, Ward worked on Beale's letters, hoping that they might contain the key. He memorized all three sets of numbers and searched in as orderly a fashion as possible in so infinite a field, for a text which would furnish him with the key. He had recognized it as a standard key-code, in which each number represented a letter in some chosen text—one of the simplest and one of the most effective of all codes. 'Each figure represented a letter,' he wrote, 'but as the numbers so greatly

Beale's Cipher No. 1—The location of the vault

71	194	38	1701	89	76	11	83	1629	48
94	63	132	16	111	95	84	341	975	14
40	64	27	81	139	213	63	90	1120	8
15	3	126	2018	40	74	758	485	604	230
436	664	582	150	251	284	308	231	124	211
486	225	401	370	11	101	305	139	189	17
33	88	208	193	145	1	94	73	416	918
263	28	500	538	356	117	136	219	27	176
130	10	460	25	485	18	436	65	84	200
283	118	320	138	36	416	280	15	71	224
961	44	16	401	39	88	61	304	12	21
24	283	134	92	63	246	486	682	7	219
184	360	780	18	64	463	474	131	160	79
73	440	95	18	64	581	34	69	128	367
460	17	81	12	103	820	62	116	97	103
862	70	60	1317	471	540	208	121	890	346
36	150	59	568	614	13	120	63	219	812
2160	1780	99	35	18	21	136	872	15	28
170	88	4	30	44	112	18	147	436	195
320	37	122	113	6	140	8	120	305	42
58	461	44	106	301	13	408	680	93	86
116	530	82	568	9	102	38	416	89	71
216	728	965	818	2	38	121	195	14	326
148	234	18	55	131	234	361	824	5	81
623	48	961	19	26	33	10	1101	365	92
88	181	275	346	201	206	86	36	219	320
829	840	68	326	19	48	122	85	216	284
919	861	326	985	233	64	68	232	431	960
50	29	81	216	321	603	14	612	81	360
36	51	62	194	78	60	200	314	676	112
4	28	18	61	136	247	819	921	1060	464
895	10	6	66	119	38	41	49	602	423
962	302	294	875	78	14	23	111	109	62
31	501	823	216	280	34	24	150	1000	162
286	19	21	17	340	19	242	31	86	234
140	607	115	33	191	67	104	86	52	88
16	80	121	67	95	122	216	548	96	11
201	77	364	218	65	667	890	236	154	211
10	98	34	119	56	216	119	71	218	1164
1496	1817	51	39	210	36	3	19	540	232
22	141	617	84	290	80	46	207	411	150
29	38	46	172	85	194	36	261	543	897
624	18	212	416	127	931	19	4	63	96
12	101	418	16	140	230	460	538	19	27
88	612	1431	90	716	275	74	83	11	426
89	72	84	1300	1706	814	221	132	40	102
34	858	975	1101	84	16	79	23	16	81
122	324	403	912	227	936	447	55	86	34
43	212	107	96	314	264	1065	323	428	601
203	124	95	216	814	2906	654	820	2	301
112	176	213	71	87	96	202	35	10	2
41	17	84	221	736	820	214	11	60	760

Beale's Cipher No. 2—The contents of the vault

115	73	24	818	37	52	49	17	31	62
657	22	7	15	140	47	29	107	79	84
56	238	10	26	822	5	195	308	85	52
159	136	59	210	36	9	46	316	543	122
106	95	53	58	2	9	47	7	35	122
31	82	77	250	195	56	96	118	71	140
287	28	353	37	994	65	147	818	24	3
8	12	47	43	59	818	45	316	101	41
78	154	994	122	138	190	16	77	49	102
57	72	34	73	85	35	371	59	195	81

The Beale Codes

92	190	106	273	60	394	629	270	219	106
388	287	63	3	6	190	122	43	233	400
106	290	314	47	48	81	96	26	115	92
157	190	110	77	85	196	46	10	113	140
353	48	120	106	2	616	61	420	822	29
125	14	20	37	105	28	248	16	158	7
35	19	301	125	110	496	287	98	117	520
62	51	219	37	113	140	818	138	549	8
44	287	388	117	18	79	344	34	20	59
520	557	107	612	219	37	66	154	41	20
50	6	584	122	154	248	110	61	52	33
30	5	38	8	14	84	57	549	216	115
71	29	85	63	43	131	29	138	47	73
238	549	52	53	79	118	51	44	63	195
12	238	112	3	49	79	353	105	56	371
566	210	515	125	360	133	143	101	15	284
549	252	14	204	140	26	822	138	115	
48	73	34	204	316	616	63	219	7	52
150	44	52	16	40	37	157	818	37	121
12	95	10	15	35	12	131	62	115	102
818	49	53	135	138	30	31	62	67	41
85	63	10	106	818	138	8	113	20	32
33	37	353	287	140	47	85	50	37	49
47	64	6	7	71	33	4	43	47	63
1	27	609	207	229	15	190	246	85	94
520	2	270	20	39	7	33	44	22	40
7	10	3	822	106	44	496	229	353	210
199	31	10	38	140	297	61	612	320	302
676	287	2	44	33	32	520	557	10	6
250	566	246	53	37	52	83	47	320	38
33	818	7	44	30	31	250	10	15	35
106	159	113	31	102	406	229	549	320	29
66	33	101	818	138	301	316	353	320	219
37	52	28	549	320	33	8	48	107	50
822	7	2	113	73	16	125	11	110	67
102	818	33	59	81	157	38	43	590	138
19	85	400	38	43	77	14	27	8	47
138	63	140	44	35	22	176	106	29	314
216	2	10	7	994	4	20	25	44	48
7	26	46	110	229	818	190	34	112	147
44	110	121	125	96	41	51	50	140	56
47	152	549	63	818	28	42	250	138	591
98	653	32	107	140	112	26	85	138	549
50	20	125	371	38	36	10	52	118	136
102	420	150	110	71	14	20	7	24	18
12	818	37	67	110	62	33	21	95	219
520	102	822	30	83	84	305	629	15	2
10	8	219	106	353	105	106	60	242	72
8	50	204	184	112	125	549	65	106	818
190	96	110	16	73	33	818	150	409	400
50	154	285	96	106	316	270	204	101	822
400	8	44	37	52	40	240	34	204	38
16	46	47	85	24	44	15	64	73	138
818	85	78	110	33	420	515	53	37	38
22	31	10	110	106	101	140	15	38	3
5	44	7	98	287	135	150	96	33	84
125	818	190	96	520	118	459	370	653	466
106	41	107	612	219	275	30	150	105	49
53	287	250	207	134	7	53	12	47	85
63	138	110	21	112	140	495	496	515	14
73	85	584	994	150	199	16	42	5	4
25	42	8	16	822	125	159	32	204	612
818	81	95	405	41	609	136	14	20	28
26	353	302	246	8	131	159	140	84	440
42	16	822	40	67	101	102	193	138	204
51	63	240	549	122	8	10	63	140	47
48	140	288							

Beale's Cipher No. 3—Names and residences of next of kin

317	8	92	73	112	89	67	318	28	96
107	41	631	78	146	397	118	98	114	246
348	116	74	88	12	65	32	14	81	19
76	121	216	85	33	66	15	108	68	77
43	24	122	96	117	36	211	301	15	44
11	46	89	18	136	68	317	28	90	82
304	71	43	221	198	176	310	319	81	99
264	380	56	37	319	2	44	53	28	44
75	98	102	37	85	107	117	64	88	136
48	151	99	175	89	315	326	78	96	214
218	311	43	89	51	90	75	128	96	33
28	103	84	65	26	41	246	84	270	98
116	32	59	74	66	69	240	15	8	121
20	77	89	31	11	106	81	191	224	328
18	75	52	82	117	201	39	23	217	27
21	84	35	54	109	128	49	77	88	1
81	217	64	55	83	116	251	269	311	96
54	32	120	18	132	102	219	211	84	150
219	275	312	64	10	106	87	75	47	21
29	37	81	44	18	126	115	132	160	181
203	76	81	299	314	337	351	96	11	28
97	318	238	106	24	93	3	19	17	26
60	73	88	14	126	138	234	286	297	321
365	264	19	22	84	56	107	98	123	111
214	136	7	33	45	40	13	28	46	42
107	196	227	344	198	203	247	116	19	8
212	230	31	6	328	65	48	52	59	41
122	33	117	11	18	25	71	36	45	83
76	89	92	31	65	70	83	96	27	33
44	50	61	24	112	136	149	176	180	194
143	171	205	296	87	12	44	51	89	98
34	41	208	173	66	9	35	16	95	8
113	175	90	56	203	19	177	183	206	157
200	218	260	291	305	618	951	320	18	124
78	65	19	32	124	48	53	57	84	96
207	244	66	82	119	71	11	86	77	213
54	82	316	245	303	86	97	106	212	18
37	15	81	89	16	7	81	39	96	14
43	216	118	29	55	109	136	172	213	64
8	227	304	611	221	364	819	375	128	296
11	18	53	76	10	15	23	19	71	84
120	134	66	73	89	96	230	48	77	26
101	127	936	218	439	178	171	61	226	313
215	102	18	167	262	114	218	66	59	48
27	19	13	82	48	162	119	34	127	139
34	128	129	74	63	120	11	54	61	73
92	180	66	75	101	124	265	89	96	126
274	896	917	434	461	235	890	312	413	328
381	96	105	217	66	118	22	77	64	42
12	7	55	24	83	67	97	109	121	135
181	203	219	228	256	21	34	77	319	374
382	675	684	717	864	203	4	18	92	16
63	82	22	46	55	69	74	112	135	186
175	119	213	416	312	343	264	119	186	218
343	417	845	951	124	209	49	617	856	924
936	72	19	29	11	35	42	40	66	85
94	112	65	82	115	119	236	244	186	172
112	85	6	56	38	44	85	72	32	47
73	96	124	217	314	319	221	644	817	821
934	922	416	975	10	22	18	46	137	181
101	39	86	103	116	138	164	212	218	296
815	380	412	460	495	675	820	952		

Note: These texts are to be read horizontally, not vertically.

exceeded the letters of the alphabet … many different numbers represented the same letter.'

At last he found one of the keys: the Declaration of Independence. By relating each number to its corresponding word and taking the first letter of each of these words, he arrived at the following statement:

> I have deposited in the County of Bedford about four miles from Bufords in an excavation or vault six feet below the surface of the ground the following articles belonging jointly to the parties whose names are given in number three herewith. The first deposit consisted of ten hundred and fourteen pounds of gold and thirty-eight hundred and twelve pounds of silver deposited November 1819. The second was made December 1821 and consisted of nineteen hundred and seven pounds of gold and twelve hundred and eighty-eight pounds of silver also jewels obtained in St Louis in exchange for silver to save transportation and valued at thirteen thousand dollars. The above is securely packed in iron pots with iron covers. The vault is roughly lined with stones and the vessels rest on solid stone and are covered with others. Paper number one describes the exact locality of the vault so that no difficulty will be had in finding it.

Ward had been on the point of giving up when he made this discovery. His obsession with the code had cost him many years, much of his health and his money, and the peace and happiness of his family. It was cruelly provocative that the first and only code that he was to break should be that which described the prize but told him nothing of the rules of the game. He returned to the quest with renewed vigour and hope, blind now to all else.

By 1885, Ward, now impoverished, remorseful and resentful, was as far from the solution as when he had begun. He gave up at last, and resolved to share the secret with the general public, hoping thereby, incidentally, to recoup some small part of his losses. He prepared a small pamphlet entitled THE BEALE PAPERS, *containing authentic statements regarding the* TREASURE BURIED *in 1819 and 1821 near Bufords, in Bedford County, Virginia*, in which he recounted the whole story and printed transcripts of all the relevant documents. Even now, Ward's luck deserted him. A fire at the printer's destroyed nearly all the copies.

We must presume here that we are not merely dealing with a cruel and elaborate hoax. It is possible, but certainly Morriss and Ward acted in good faith, and, from all that we know of Beale, there is no reason to suppose that he would have thus wantonly—and at great expense of time and money—have left such a malign legacy. Such a find as that of Beale's party is by no means inconceivable, and there are auriferous hills to the North of Santa Fe. That all thirty claimants should have died so soon seems at first sight implausible, but it must be recalled that these men travelled as a party and sought their wealth in hostile Indian country. No doubt all or many of them were still with Beale when he wrote his last letter to Morriss in May 1822.

The two encoded messages yet to be deciphered, Ciphers 1 and 3, must be assumed to be in a key-code similar to that of Cipher 2. No. 1, we are told gives the location of the vault. No. 3 contains the names of the claimants and names and addresses of all the beneficiaries. Here we come upon an intriguing point. There are little more than six hundred numbers in this paper. If each number represents one letter, as in Cipher 2, we are to believe that two names and one address are contained in an average space of twenty letters, or, to put it another way, that no item of information averages more than seven letters. Even so short a name and so terse an address as, say, 'John Smith, Denver' contains fifteen characters and is, so to speak, over the limit.

It therefore seems likely to me that we are dealing here with one of two possible sophistications of the basic key code. The numbers given (they start, for example '317, 8, 92, 73, 112 …') may in fact be intended to be read as single digits or in units of two, and the commas may merely be designed to increase confusion—a common enough trick in key codes. Alternatively, Beale may have been using some sort of local directory as a key. If this was so then a list of electors, in which names such as 'John' or 'Denver' or whatever frequently recur seems the most likely possibility. I personally favour the former theory, which would mean that this key were limited to a maximum of one hundred words and a minimum of ten.

FURTHER ACTION

The keys must plainly, like the Declaration of Independence, have been readily attainable to citizens of Virginia at the time of their composition. They might, of course, simply be prayers, rhymes or some such widely memorized texts.

Cipher 3 may, of course, be approached from another angle. A certain number of assumptions may be made concerning the contents of this paper. Names of Beale's comrades may yet be traced by the researcher, and we can expect to find repeated references to Richmond and other Virginia towns.

The Beale codes will be deciphered one day, and I cannot recommend that the treasure-seeker hunts elsewhere than in these long lists of numbers. The full text of *The Beale Papers* can be had from The Beale Cypher Association (P.O. Box 236, Warrington, Pennsylvania, PA18976, USA). Luck will play as great a part as assiduity or skill in the solution of the mystery.

An ingenious associate instantly suggested on hearing the story of the codes that, if the second of the codes has the Declaration of Independence as its key and is thus associated with Jefferson, the key to the first will be Thomas (Thomas Paine seems the obvious candidate, but the gospel of the pseudo-evangelist Thomas may also reward study) and that to the third will be Beale or some pun on the name. I have not had leisure to test this theory, but it is certainly very attractive. Any educated guess of this sort may solve the riddle that has resisted solution now for more than a century.

PLAZUELA MONASTERY, COCHABAMBA, BOLIVIA
BURIED JESUIT RICHES

In 1767, Charles III, king of Spain, ordered the expulsion of all Jesuits from Bolivia. They had become too powerful and, for all their wealth, deemed that they need only render unto God what was God's and keep Caesar's portion for themselves. The Royal Fifth, a tax levied on all New World treasures, had been ignored by the Jesuits for many years. There had even been rumours that they intended to establish a South American colony independent of Spain.

The Jesuits of Plazuela may have doubted that the deportation order would ever be enforced. They were virtually emperors in their remote, afforested region and probably thought themselves unassailable. They soon had evidence of the seriousness of the threat, however, when the Spanish authorities mounted a blockade of the mountain passes, rendering it impossible for them to import supplies or to send out gold.

Since 1635 or a little later, Plazuela had been a central depot for the product of neighbouring mines of well nigh fabulous richness, including the Tres Tertillas and El Carmen. In the course of the past century it had become perhaps the richest of all the rich seminaries in Latin America.

Concluding that their deportation was inevitable, the priests resolved that their mineral wealth at least should not fall into profane hands. Five hundred Indian labourers are known to have been recruited at this time. The bodies of three hundred of these labourers who died of fever are thought to be buried in a neighbouring hill. Local legend also reveres another spot nearby as a mass grave. It may be idle and irresponsible to suggest, on such slender evidence, that the good fathers of Plazuela murdered their servants when their job was done, but there would have been little point in having such work done at all if all those who knew of it were not either sworn to secrecy in a mutual interest, or dead.

Eleven years after the deportation order, bemused Spanish soldiers arrived at Plazuela to carry out their king's wishes. They found the seminary deserted and stripped of all its riches. Interrogation of some few unfortunate Indians, even with torture, extracted no solution to the mystery. The soldiers returned empty-handed.

The Prodgers Expedition

The story of the Jesuit treasure, supposedly—and presumably—buried somewhere near the site of the seminary, did not die. We know of at least two expeditions to Plazuela in the following century, one under the auspices of the then president, General Mariano Melgarejo. Even officialdom had acknowledged by then that the Jesuit wealth must be hidden somewhere, but these expeditions laboured under one serious disadvantage—an erroneous tradition, created and fostered perhaps by the devious monks, as to the supposed location of the treasure.

It was not until 1904 that the true facts emerged. Cecil H. Prodgers, a well-known mining engineer, was approached by the daughter of a former president of Peru with an intriguing proposition. Corina San Roman told Prodgers—and he quickly confirmed—that her grandfather had been the youngest brother of one of the last eight Jesuits of Plazuela. In 1778, when Prefect of Callao, he had been visited by his departing brother, Father Gregorio San Roman, who left him a description of the treasure's hiding-place:

> There is a hill on the left bank of the Rio Sacambaya opposite the Monastery of Plazuela. It is steep and covered with dense forest. The top is flat and with long grass growing. In the middle of the long

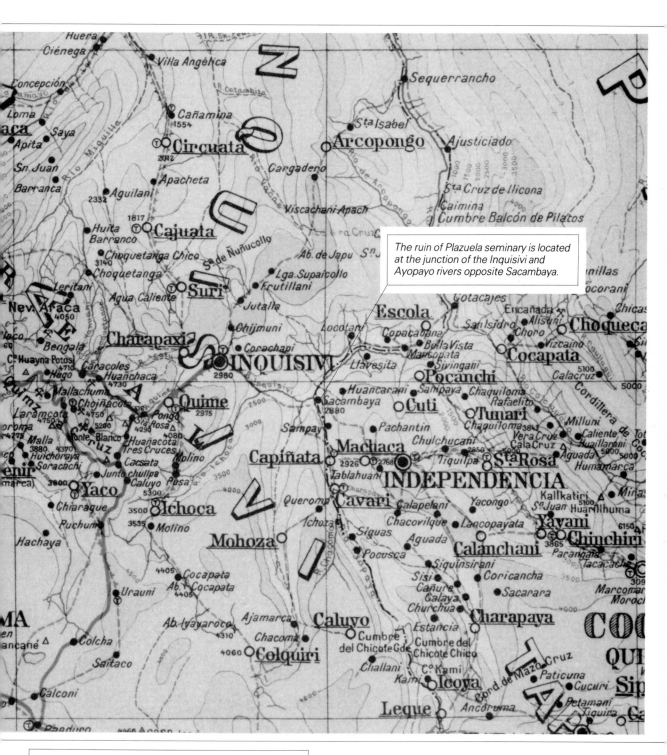

The ruin of Plazuela seminary is located at the junction of the Inquisivi and Ayopayo rivers opposite Sacambaya.

Map of part of Cochabamba Province, Bolivia, reproduced from a 1933 Bolivian Government map. Scale approximately 1:4,000,000.

grass there is a large stone shaped like an egg, so big that it took five hundred Indians to place it there. If you dig underneath this stone for five *cordas* you will find the roof of a large cave which it took five hundred Indians two and a half years to hollow out. The roof is twenty-four *cordas* long and there are two compartments and a long narrow passage leading from the room on the east side to the main entrance two hundred *cordas* away. On reaching the door you must exercise great care in opening. The door is a large iron one and inside to the right, near the wall, you will find an image of the Madonna,

made of pure gold, three feet high, the eyes of which are two large diamonds; this image was placed there for the good of mankind. If you proceed along the passage you will find in the first room 37 heaps of gold, and many gold and silver ornaments and precious stones. On entering the second room you will find in the right-hand corner a large box clamped with iron bars; inside this box are 90,000 *duros reales* in silver money and 30 bags of gold. Distributed in the hollows on either side of the tunnel and in the two rooms are, altogether, 160 heaps of gold, of which the value has been estimated at 60 million *duros reales*. Great care must be taken on entering these rooms, as enough poison to kill a regiment of the King has been laid about. The walls of the two rooms have been strengthened by large blocks of granite; from the roof downwards the distance is five *cordas* more. The top of the roof is portioned off in three distinct esplanades and the whole has been covered for a depth of five *cordas* with earth and stone.

When you come to a place twenty feet high, with a wall so wide that two men can easily ride abreast, cross the river and you will find the monastery,

Left: The valley of the River Inquisivi, where it is joined by the Ayopaya just beside the ruins of the monastery of Plazuela. In one of the hills in this photograph, the Jesuits spent over two years hiding a fortune in gold, silver and precious stones before their expulsion from South America at the end of the eighteenth century.

Stratford Jolly's sketch-map shows all the key sites at Plazuela. It should be noted that the names of the rivers have changed several times during this century.

church and other buildings.
[The *corda* is an old Spanish measure supposed to be equivalent to 22 ft. 7 ins.]

Corina San Roman suggested to Prodgers that they should share the treasure, if he would do the work of finding it. He agreed to this and shortly after set off armed with the name of an old Indian whom the San Romans had long paid to watch over the site but who had not been heard of for eight years. This old man, José Maria Ampuera, was well over 100, and living in the village of Cuti, where Prodgers found him in 1905. He was the grandson of one of those who had helped the Jesuits hide the treasure. From a wealthy family, he had a long-standing grudge against the Bolivian authorities on the grounds of previous

ill-treatment and for this reason had refrained from correcting President Melgarejo's error in searching for the treasure on the hill called Negro Muerto, or Dead Negro, on the wrong side of the River Sacambaya. The true site, to which he was only too happy to lead Prodgers when he knew that he represented the interests of the San Romans, was the hill called Caballo Cunco. Negro Muerto was in fact the mass grave of those Indian builders said to have died of fever.

José waited at the bottom as Prodgers climbed the hill. To his delight, Prodgers at once found the big, egg-shaped stone described in the document. As soon as he had obtained permission from the government to work the site, he dynamited the stone, which was 15 ft. high and 14 ft. in diameter. Beneath it he found a man-

The adobe walls of the Jesuit mission showing holes left by recent treasure hunters. Other ruins are nearby.

made roof of bricks and slate slabs, 75 ft. long and 30 ft. broad. He started to dig at the southernmost end. Later he wrote that there

> I found the bones of birds, guinea-pigs, some snail shells that are generally found on trees, and stones and pebbles from the river beach below, and when, at the depth of 9 feet, I picked up a wooden cork, and, at 12 feet, a yellow altar slab with flowers nicely engraved on it, there was no longer any doubt in my mind...'

He also learned that the Indian owner of Caballo Cunco had found some £20,000 on the hill over the course of many years. As José came to trust Prodgers, he revealed that he and his sons had found a golden bell weighing 40 lbs. a few years before Melgarejo's expedition, although Prodgers does not tell us where.

All this was heartening, but five *cordas* is a long way to dig. By the end of 1907, after three seasons' searching, a number of exciting adventures and two narrow escapes from death—including an occasion when, on sinking a bamboo shoot into the hillside and striking something soft, a noxious gas was released—Prodgers had nothing to show for all his efforts but a quantity of silver plate uncovered in one of the old burial mounds close to the river. The superstitions of the Indians had constantly hampered his investigations. He returned to England, resolved to muster a more sceptical workforce, but he was never to come back to Plazuela.

The Continuing Search

In 1913 an unnamed Cornishman tried to involve Colonel Fawcett, the explorer, in a hunt for the Plazuela treasure. Fawcett visited the site and found plenty of evidence of previous searches, but his true interests lay elsewhere, and he declined to spend his time or money there. This Cornishman claimed to have partnered an Englishman previously. If this partner was Prodgers, then the Cornishman must be the tiresome and tireless Tredennick, who from 1921 to 1927 worked at Plazuela on his own account, constructing many tunnels and galleries in Caballo Cunco. His most significant achievement in that time was the

The Square Stone Heap was a huge, artificial and perfectly rectangular structure of stone 618 ft. by 128 ft., discovered on Caballo Cunco, a hill at Plazuela, during Sanders' first expedition in 1925–6. Sanders believed treasure lay below it.

unfortunate dynamiting of a mineshaft, after which there was a tremendous internal upheaval lasting an hour and a half. Tredinnick is said to have persevered for as long as he did on the advice of a Hindu Yogi.

Prodgers died in 1923, but in 1920 he had passed on his knowledge to a mining expert, Dr Edgar Sanders, on the single condition that Sanders would honour Prodgers' liability to Corina San Roman.

Sanders organized a small expedition in 1925 and examined the whole of the hill systematically over that and the following season. He made two discoveries. About 900 ft. down the hillside from the site of the egg-shaped stone he found a huge, artificial and perfectly rectangular structure of stone, 618 ft. by 128 ft., subsequently known as the Square Stone Heap. Exactly opposite the seminary ruins, at a little distance from the Heap, he found a tunnel.

The silver crucifix found by Sanders in a tunnel lying exactly opposite the ruins of the monastery. With it was a piece of parchment, the text of which began: 'You who reach this place withdraw...'

piece of parchment lay inside the box in a good state of preservation. It had one side of writing, all in Spanish except for the last sentence which was Latin. Sanders painstakingly read out the text in the presence of the Indian workers who were with him:

> You who reach this place withdraw. This spot is dedicated to God Almighty and the one who dares to enter, a dolorous death awaits him in this world and eternal condemnation in the world he goes to. The riches that belong to God Our Master are not for humans. Withdraw and you will live in peace and the blessing of the Master will make your life sweet and you will die rich with the goods of this world. Obey the command of God Almighty our Master in life and in death. In the name of God the Father, the Son and the Holy Ghost. Amen.

Sanders was, it would seem, on the very threshold of the treasure cave, but he had made a fatal mistake in reading his text aloud. The Indians, filled with superstitious fear, refused to do any further work in the tunnel. With the rainy season nearly upon them, Sanders had to halt operations for that year.

Sanders had spent many thousands of pounds already in the course of his search, but his hopes were running high. Back in England he had a pamphlet published as a first step towards the formation of a syndicate capable of equipping a new expedition to its greatest strength. Eventually £20,000 was raised, making possible the purchase of 45 tons of equipment including four drill compressors, two electric generators, six cranes, two Morris six-wheel tractors, a hydraulic pump, and a big marquee measuring 30 ft. by 50 ft. In March 1928 Sanders and twenty-two others sailed out of Liverpool.

The party started work on 15 June and spent the first ten days removing the thick, wet earth from the tunnel. To their astonishment and dismay, it turned out to be a dead end. Although it might, of course, have been a preliminary attempt and there may be another tunnel leading into the Heap, Sanders was convinced that it was a Jesuit red herring intended to mislead seekers.

They next searched the ancient ruined fortress which stood at the same distance from the Heap as the original tunnel, but there was no sign of any

Sanders believed the Heap to be the roof of the cave containing the treasure, but first he began to clear the tunnel which had been completely filled with earth. Sanders reckoned that Father San Roman's document had not been written by the Father at all but by his brother trying to record everything he had heard him say. He was convinced that the egg-shaped stone was only a marker, and that in other respects the document was not to be trusted on points of detail.

A few days' digging in the tunnel turned up a board, to which was nailed a silver crucifix. Four yards beyond, his party found a wall of loose stones completely blocking the tunnel. There was a hole within this wall, and in the hole a small wooden box that fell to pieces in his hands. A

other tunnel entrance, so they turned their attention to the Heap itself. They dug directly downward in search of the treasure cave, but hit virgin rock in late July. A mood of despondency set in. The hill—their area of search—was simply too large. Each of the landmarks offered such promise that on each occasion they were left more downcast when their hopes were dashed after weeks of hard work.

Their stay was not entirely fruitless. They relieved their frustration by exploring other sites in the neighbourhood. They visited, for example, the cave, three hours ride away, where the skeletons of a further three hundred Indians lay, and the priory of Cuticutini, just a mile from the ruined fortress on the other side of the River Sacambaya, where gold relics had been found beneath a chapel altar. A visiting geologist who accompanied them to Monte Sapo, a gold mine close to Cuticutini, pronounced it to be very rich.

All this confirmed what they knew and corroborated their suspicions. The Jesuits had been working immensely rich mines. It was inconceivable that, despite the blockades, they had somehow contrived to spirit all their wealth in coin, church plate and bullion across the mountains and sea to Spain. It must therefore be somewhere near the seminary. A large number of Indians had died at the same time and in the same place. There were extensive workings within the hill. The treasure must be somewhere there.

Sanders's conviction that the Heap must be the focal point of their search was strengthened by a piece of intelligence from their blacksmith. He told them that, in 1927, a party of Turks or Armenians had scoured Plazuela, Negro Muerto and Caballo Cunco with a metal detector but had received no positive response save at the Heap. As if to tantalize them further, a very old Indian came forward to state that his father had been present when the Jesuits were carrying out extensive work on that spot. There were three iron doors, he said, in a passage which led to the treasure chamber.

At last, with the coming of the rains, work had to be halted. 'I could not tell you how I feel,' wrote Sanders, 'Heartbroken is a very mild word for it. There are moments when I feel that my hair has gone white.' Refusing to pay protection money to an influential extortionist he was the last member of the expedition to leave Bolivia. At length he was forced to concede and buy his way out. Over eight months, he and his party had shifted nearly 40,000 tons of rock to no avail.

The Recent Evidence

Apart from a lone American who spent two years on the site and found nothing and three Bolivians from Cochabamba, one of whom, so local legend has it, dreamed one night of treasure, got up to dig for it and was found by his companions the next morning clutching two gold goblets and totally mad, no one seems to have visited Caballo Cunco until the mid-1960s, when two television reporters, Tony Morrison and Mark Howell, arrived with a sophisticated metal detector capable of detecting metal to a depth of twenty feet. They intended merely to reconnoitre with a view to a more serious investigation in years to come. Unfortunately they chose the rainy season.

'The journey was everything we had expected,' wrote Mark Howell later, 'earthslides, cataracts across the road, the shoulders of bends washed away. We went through rain, hail and finally snow on the Cumbre, and then in more torrential rain we slithered the forty tortuous miles down to Quime. The last part, a steep, twisting descent of four thousand feet, we covered in the dark.'

When at last they arrived safely at the site, they established that the soil was ideally suited to their metal detector. They knew of a story that the Jesuits had sealed the entrance to a tunnel by diverting the river across the entrance. This encouraged them to perform tests on the sandbank bordering the true bank of the river, but with little or no joy. They also searched the little chapel where the demented Bolivian is meant to have found the goblets. The most interesting discoveries here were some tiny clay pots, posies of wild flowers, food scraps and the burned bones of a guinea-pig, all placed there as offerings within the last week: clear proof that this site, although many miles from even the meanest Indian settlement, was still visited and retained some significance.

Morrison and Howell next climbed a hill which they believed to be Caballo Cunco, expecting to find the egg-shaped stone on top. But the hill, only 400 ft. high, was clearly not Caballo Cunco, which is over twice that height, nor, even had it been, would the stone have been more than a fragment of what it was.

On the other side of the river they searched the remains of various buildings including a church. Here, 5 yards from a ruined house, Howell located a metal object some 4½ ft. underground and about 20 in. square. He eagerly brought the news to his partner only to be told that they must immediately leave. The rains were starting. They dug frantically and, just as the first drops of the downpour fell, unearthed an ancient trapezoid copper plate with three holes in it. It weighed four pounds. Although unimportant in itself, it served to convince them (erroneously, if we believe Sanders) that theirs was the first metal detector to

This heavy piece of copper plate was discovered at Plazuela by Mark Howell using a metal detector. He located it just as the rains were starting to fall and barely had time to retrieve it before being obliged, with his fellow-searcher, Tony Morrison, to flee the valley.

Mark Howell was one of the two explorers who visited Plazuela in the mid-1960s. An expert in geophysical prospecting, he is shown here with a prototype metal detector.

have been used on the site. For the moment, however, they had only one concern—to escape from the valley as fast as possible.

Having learned to their cost the perils and the futility of a random search of so wide and so hostile an area, the two reporters resolved on a more circumspect and investigative style of enquiry on their subsequent visit. They talked with several Indians who claimed to possess the secret of the treasure's location. These they did not take too seriously, but far more interesting was an ancient and beautifully inscribed document shown to them by a Bolivian friend. This document purported to give the hiding-places of quantities of gold and church plate. Various landmarks, none of which the pair could identify—were given as points of reference, and the most striking indication—the shadow thrown by the church-tower at midday on midsummer's day—is, as they surmise, hardly likely to be helpful. The author of the document was perhaps only too correct in his pessimistic prophesy: 'In a thousand years, the chambers could never be found'.

FURTHER ACTION

As previous searchers have discovered, and as the illustrations show, the Sacambaya valley is so steep-sided that though it is possible to enter during the rainy season, it is perilous to leave in view of landslides and mudslips. To stand any chance of success, the modern treasure hunter must prepare a small expedition, equipped for a lengthy stay in light jungle over the summer months.

However untrustworthy Father Gregorio's document may be, there is enough evidence—for example, Sanders's silver crucifix—to suggest the site is worth further exploration, preferably using advanced sensory equipment to search for another tunnel. Mark Howell, now a geophysical expert, who has not had the opportunity to return to the site, has spent the last six or seven years researching a new machine capable of analysing underground shapes and contours by means of a vibratory technique.

Although further research in literary material would be less productive than usual, C. H. Prodgers's *Adventures in Bolivia* and Stratford Jolly's *The Treasure Trail* give good accounts of the Prodgers and Sanders expeditions respectively. There are other works on Sanders's expeditions by Ralph Stead and T. C. Bridges.

RENNES-LE-CHÂTEAU, AUDE, FRANCE

A VISIGOTHIC OR MEROVINGIAN HOARD

The mysteries of Rennes-le-Château have now attained cult status, not least because, like the Beale codes, they constitute a series of codified riddles which may apparently be as easily solved by the amateur in his office or his sitting-room as by the professional in the field. Whilst the Beale codes, however, are simple enough in nature, the riddles of Rennes-le-Château are—or at least have been made to seem—labyrinthine in their complexity. In their now famous bestseller *The Holy Blood and the Holy Grail*, Michael Baigent, Richard Leigh and Henry Lincoln have mixed heresy and high politics, great names from history, dynasties, secret societies, cryptic writings and paintings and a whole pot-pourri of intriguing ingredients which seem somehow, elusively, connected.

This, however, is a book for treasure hunters, and there can be no doubt that Rennes-le-Château is, or has been, the hiding place of a substantial treasure and considerable wealth. Baigent *et al.* conclude that this treasure is the royal blood, the *sang réal* of the Merovingian dynasty which they ingeniously identify with the Holy Grail. They further conclude that this blood—this royal succession—is all the more important and dangerous to the European *status quo* because the Merovingian kings are directly descended from Jesus and his wife, whom they tentatively identify as the Magdalene. All this is enchanting and tantalizing stuff, but our first concern must be to distinguish facts from speculation.

Village History

Rennes-le-Château is a tiny village of two hundred inhabitants. It crowns a hilltop in a remote and beautiful region of Southern France. Wandering down its narrow main street, it is hard to conceive that this was once an important, bustling centre and the home of 30,000 people. Here, in the fifth century, the Visigoths established a large, well-fortified settlement. With Carcassonne as their main base, they then went on to subdue the whole of Roman Gaul.

Another tribe, the Franks, in time expelled the Visigoths from the greater part of France. The Visigoths withdrew to what was later to become the kingdom of Septimania, a large area in the south-east which included Rhedae, as Rennes-le-Château was then called. Amalaric, one of their kings, is said to have given Rhedae the status of Royal City after his marriage to a Frankish princess, and for a while it could compare with Carcassonne itself.

Long after the Visigoth power had faded, Rennes was still prospering. Its decline dates from the decision of Ermengarde, an eleventh-century noblewoman, to sell the earldom of Razès (of which Rennes was the centre) to the House of Barcelona. Although her grandsons later reclaimed it, its status as a Royal City was lost forever.

In the following centuries, it was twice demolished and twice restored before finally it was devastated by plague and by the Routiers, notorious looters, commanded by the ferocious Henri, Earl of Trastamare, in the 1360s.

History then passed by Rennes-le-Château. It retained some small significance by reason of its mineral wealth. Lamoignon de Basville informs us that mines in the neighbouring mountain had been worked since Roman times. Gensanne, forty years later, is more specific, stating that copper, lead and silver are to be found 'especially in the mountains of Cardun and Roquenègre'. He also refers to the rumours of a gold and silver mine on Blanchefort Mountain.

Whatever riches the mountains contained had been exhausted by about 1600 and De Basville could write: '*Soit que les mines aient été epuisées ou que l'art de les trouver se soit perdu, les tresors, si il'y en a, sont maintenant si cachés que l'on ne pense plus a les chercher.*' ('Whether the mines have been exhausted or the art of finding them lost, such treasures as there may be are now so hidden that one no longer thinks of looking for them.')

Gérard de Sède writing in 1967 added to this: '*le filon d'or, orienté sud-nord et long de cinquante mètres, se trouve sur les parcelles 625 et 626 de la section A du cadastre; jadis, ce filon commençait à fleur de terre sur la parcelle 633.*' ('The vein of gold, orientated south to north and fifty metres long, is on parts 625 and 626 of section A of the land register; once, this vein started from the earth's surface on part 33.')

The Merovingian Mystery

The second set of facts concerns the Merovingian succession and the Priory of Sion. The last Merovingian king (the Merovingian dynasty ruled over the Franks), Dagobert II, was treacherously murdered by some of his leading subjects in 679. This is almost the only solidly documented evidence we have in a passage of French history renowned for its obscurity.

The Priory of Sion is, or pretends to be, an ancient secret society. As early as 1116, we have a charter signed by a Prior of the order of Notre Dame de Sion. The order's origins are obscure, but it is reasonable to suppose that it was one of the many orders of warlike holy men which were formed during the Crusades. Piety was not the only motive for their formation. The legendary wealth of the East drew many Europeans to enrol in what, in effect, were often little more than bands of adventurers bound by rituals and licensed by the Pope. From the very beginning it seems that the order of Notre Dame de Sion was associated with the notorious Knights Templar.

The Priory of Sion, whether directly descended from the earlier order, or merely taking its name, survives in the present day, boasting many distinguished initiates. Of late, under cover of a whole series of impenetrable pseudonyms, it has been 'coming out', as it were, gradually releasing information as to its ultimate ends. Its members maintain that Dagobert's little son, Sigisbert, was not, as is generally believed, killed with his father, but escaped with his sister's help to his mother Giselle's home in Razès. In due course, if this were so, he would have inherited his uncle's estates and titles and thus established a covert royal dynasty.

We know that Dagobert did indeed have a son. However, Giselle, his supposed second wife, seems to be unknown to history. The one document which might have supported the Priory's claims—a charter dated 718 recording the foundation of a monastery by 'Sigebert, Comte de Rhédae and his wife Magdala' has not so far been traced.

The identification of a Merovingian claimant to the throne of France would today be regarded as an interesting historical curiosity, but no more politically significant than, say, the claims of an Anglo-Saxon heir to the throne of England and Scotland. It seems, indeed, that we already know the identity of the supposed heir. Why, then, is his claim backed by a powerful and wealthy secret society whose secrecy remains inviolate?

The Priory is supposed to have some knowledge very damaging to orthodox Christianity. The authors of *The Holy Blood and the Holy Grail* put forward a case to suggest that either Jesus escaped execution and came to France or elsewhere, or that his wife and children arrived in Marseilles soon after the crucifixion and that Dagobert was Jesus's direct descendant. This of course ties in with an ancient European tradition that the Magdalene did flee to France, just as Joseph of Arimathea is said to have come to England. The case for the reinstatement of the Magdalene as a respectable figure is an interesting one. But can we believe this story and, even if we do—or if the members of the Priory do—by what means could it ever be proved and how damaging would it ultimately prove to orthodox Christianity?

Whatever the Priory's secrets, we are concerned here not with bloodlines but with actual treasure. It seems beyond doubt that,

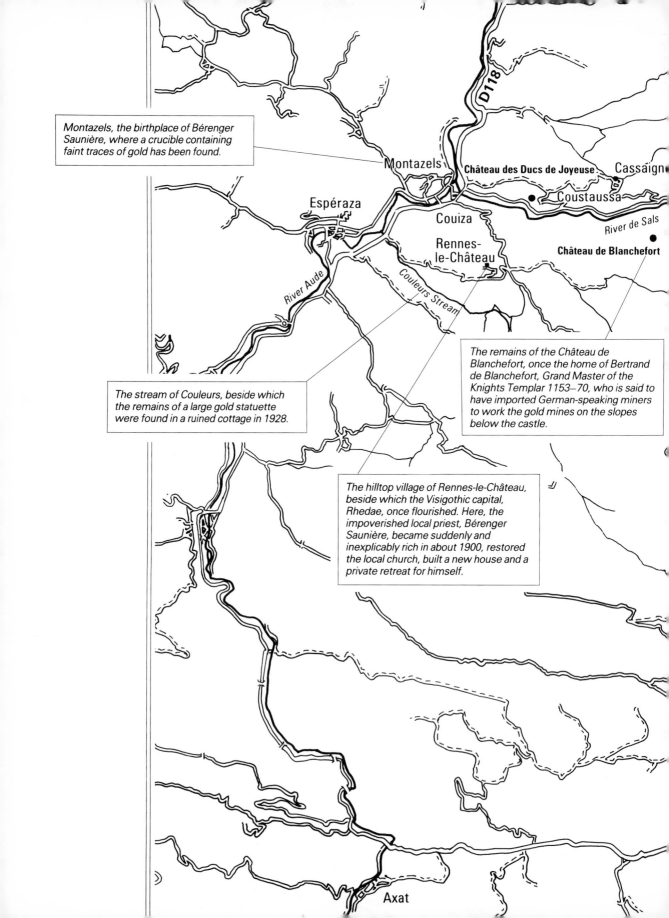

Montazels, the birthplace of Bérenger Saunière, where a crucible containing faint traces of gold has been found.

Montazels

Château des Ducs de Joyeuse

Cassaign

Coustaussa

Espéraza

Couiza

Rennes-le-Château

River de Sals

Château de Blanchefort

River Aude

Couleurs Stream

The stream of Couleurs, beside which the remains of a large gold statuette were found in a ruined cottage in 1928.

The remains of the Château de Blanchefort, once the home of Bertrand de Blanchefort, Grand Master of the Knights Templar 1153–70, who is said to have imported German-speaking miners to work the gold mines on the slopes below the castle.

The hilltop village of Rennes-le-Château, beside which the Visigothic capital, Rhedae, once flourished. Here, the impoverished local priest, Bérenger Saunière, became suddenly and inexplicably rich in about 1900, restored the local church, built a new house and a private retreat for himself.

Axat

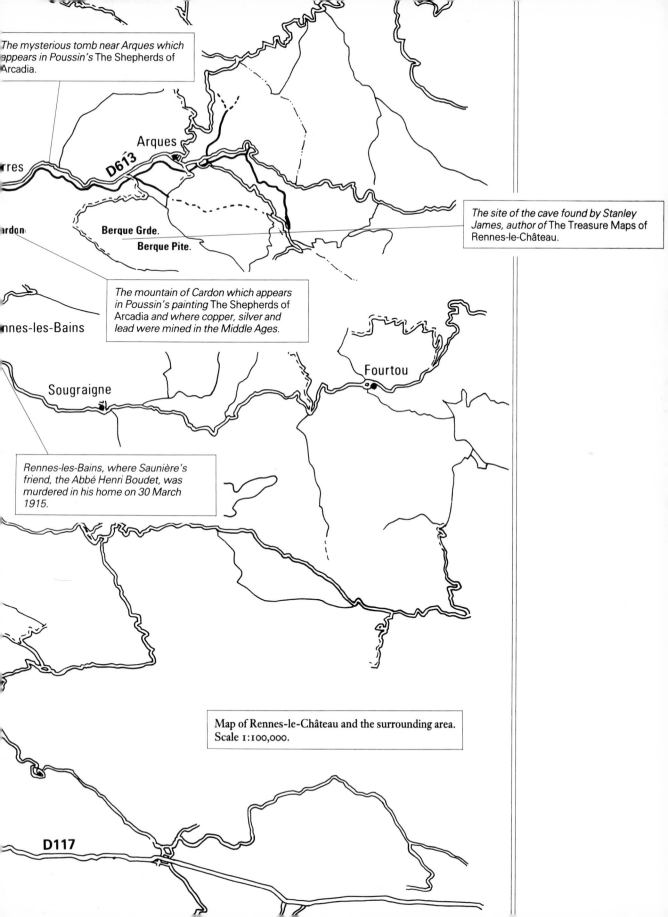

The mysterious tomb near Arques which appears in Poussin's The Shepherds of Arcadia.

Arques

D613

rres

ardon

Berque Grde.
Berque Pite.

The site of the cave found by Stanley James, author of The Treasure Maps of Rennes-le-Château.

The mountain of Cardon which appears in Poussin's painting The Shepherds of Arcadia and where copper, silver and lead were mined in the Middle Ages.

nnes-les-Bains

Fourtou

Sougraigne

Rennes-les-Bains, where Saunière's friend, the Abbé Henri Boudet, was murdered in his home on 30 March 1915.

Map of Rennes-le-Château and the surrounding area.
Scale 1:100,000.

D117

notwithstanding the real or supposed secrets of the Priory of Sion, there has been and may still be a treasure of great worth in the immediate area of Rennes-le-Château.

The Priest and his Codes

In 1891, the curé of Rennes-le-Château suddenly and inexplicably became enormously rich.

Bérenger Saunière was thirty-nine in that year. A burly extrovert, distinguished more by his energy than his culture, he was a keen hunter and fisherman. He was unquestionably an ambitious man, however, and had cultivated the classical tongues.

Three years before, Saunière had started the renovation of his church. Dedicated to Mary Magdalene over eight hundred years before, the little church was in grave need of repair. Now

In 1891 Bérenger Saunière, an obscure French country priest, discovered some manuscripts hidden in his parish church. Soon after, he became extremely rich, but no one has ever established the source of his wealth. Evidence suggests a great treasure of ancient origin lay, and perhaps still lies, hidden in the neighbourhood.

Saunière ordered that an altar stone should be lifted off two Visigothic columns. One of these columns proved to be hollow. It contained four wooden cylinders sealed with wax. Each cylinder contained a parchment. Saunière at once set to work to make sense of them.

Two of the documents were immediately and easily comprehensible. One purported to be the genealogy of the Earls of Razès up to 1244. It claimed that they were directly descended from the Merovingian kings. It bore the seal of Blanche de Castille, Queen of France. A second parchment, the will of François-Pierre d'Hautpoul, Lord of Rennes and Bézu, continued the genealogy from 1244 to 1644.

The remaining two documents were baffling. They appeared to be no more than inaccurate and rather garbled Latin versions of two New Testament stories. One text was based on Luke VI, I–IV, and other parallel texts, in which Jesus is criticized by the Pharisees for working on the Sabbath. The second (John XII, I–XI) concerns Jesus's visit to the house of Mary and Martha, the sisters of Lazarus, in Bethany. Whether that Mary is also the Magdalene is unclear. The incomprehensible feature of these manuscripts was that one hundred and forty totally superfluous letters had been written into the text. Words ran one into the other. Letters were raised or lines mysteriously shortened. Saunière recognized that he was dealing with ciphers, and acknowledged that he did not possess the scholarship or the skills to crack them. He consulted his bishop, who paid his expenses to Paris and advised that he consult certain notable scholars of the church, including one young and brilliant linguist named Emile Hoffet, who was well known for his interest in the occult and the hermetic tradition.

During his three weeks in Paris, Saunière was introduced into Hoffet's wide circle of friends. Emma Calvé, the famous opera singer was widely rumoured to have become the priest's lover. She certainly became a close friend and frequently visited Saunière at Rennes-le-Château in the years to come. Why this brilliant *diva* should have been so interested in an unprepossessing provincial curé is not known. It must be remembered, however, that *fin de siècle* opera singers were not renowned for their virtue—Calvé was well known for her numerous liaisons—and that *demi-mondaines* could readily, if expensively, be bought and sold, for a nobleman's son, for example, or perhaps for a priest who had come up with an embarrassing secret and must now be flattered, cajoled and seduced into silence.

When Saunière returned from the capital, it seems that he understood the messages of the ciphers and, furthermore, that he appreciated their precise significance. The raised letters of the first text, taken in order (but discounting the first line) spelled out:

This is one of the two coded documents discovered in 1891 by Bérenger Saunière during repairs to his church. It is a Latin version of one of the New Testament stories, but 140 extra letters have been added, which, taken separately, form a complex cipher for a strange text.

A DAGOBERT II ROI ET SION EST CE TRESOR ET IL EST LA MORT

Baigent, Leigh and Lincoln translate this as 'To Dagobert II, King, and to Sion belongs this treasure and he is there dead'—a highly implausible interpretation. Far more likely and far more literal is the warning: 'TO DAGOBERT II, KING, AND TO SION BELONGS THIS TREASURE, AND IT IS DEATH.' Interestingly, Lincoln includes both translations in an early article on the subject, but omits the second one in *The Holy Blood and the Holy Grail*.

The second text was dauntingly difficult to decode. 128 of the 140 extra letters had to be laid out according to the well-known Vigenère cipher system, and a key phrase applied, producing a second set of letters. This set was also substituted according to a new pattern; then a new key had to be applied; then two further substitutions had to be made. Then the new set of letters was laid out in a pattern corresponding to two chess boards. An imaginary knight then moved across the boards and produced the final text. It is inconceivable that this technique could have been discovered and applied in the space of three weeks unless the person or persons who did so already knew the key. This argues that, although the manuscripts had been hidden for one hundred years, they were coded according to a known, arcane principle. This further argues the existence of a society or order in which such a convention was known and had survived for centuries.

The passage which emerged from this tortuous process reads as follows:

BERGERE PAS DE TENTATION QUE POUSSIN TENIERS GARDENT LA CLEF PAX DCLXXXI PAR LA CROIX ET CE CHEVAL DE DIEU J'ACHEVE CE DAEMON DE GARDIEN A MIDI POMMES BLEUES

The literal translation—if a literal translation is what is needed—runs: SHEPHERDESS NO TEMP-TATION [or, improbably, steps of temptation] THAT POUSSIN TENIERS KEEP THE KEY PEACE 681 [or perhaps 500, 100, 50, 10, 10, 10, 1] BY [or through] THE CROSS AND THIS HORSE OF GOD I ATTAIN THIS DEMON GUARDIAN AT NOON BLUE APPLES

This seventeenth-century painting by Nicolas Poussin is believed to be very important to the story of Rennes-le-Château. A reference to Poussin in a ciphered document found there, the fact of Saunière's possession of a copy of the painting, its unusual geometric scheme, Poussin's claim to knowledge of a great secret, and the existence of a similar tomb near Arques, not far from the village are amongst the reasons for thinking so.

Saunière's Paintings

Saunière returned to Rennes-le-Château with reproductions of three paintings which he clearly believed to be related to this text. One was a portrait of Célestin, an obscure thirteenth-century hermit pope. Another may have been *Saint Anthony and Saint Jerome in the Desert* by David Teniers—either the older or the younger. The last was Nicolas Poussin's *The Shepherds of Arcadia*.

The Flemish painter David Teniers the Elder lived from 1582 to 1649, his son from 1610 to 1690. Nicolas Poussin (1593/4–1665) was thus their contemporary. We cannot be sure in which Teniers painting Saunière was so interested, nor whether he picked on the right canvas. There are more than two thousand works attributed to Teniers the Younger alone—many falsely. As to Poussin, however, there are indications that the painting—in the version supposedly used by Saunière—has a bearing on the mystery of Rennes-le-Château.

First, the whole painting is constructed around a regular pentagon, from which may be formed a pentacle whose centre lies directly above the shepherdess's head. Second, the landscape, so far from being imaginary as was formerly assumed, vaguely resembles a point six miles to the east of Rennes-le-Château. All the rock formations there correspond with those in the painting, including the peak of Cardou, which is to the right of the trees and to the left of the smaller and more distant mount of Rennes-le-Château. Even the stone in front of the tomb and the tree (*quercus ilex*) behind it are supposed to be found on the site.

The tomb itself also exists and can be seen near Arques. It is said on rather doubtful authority to have been there in 1709. It was opened in the 1920s and found, curiously, to be empty. Two Americans have since been buried there.

The simplest explanation for this course of events is based on the legend on the tomb in Poussin's painting, '*Et in Arcadia Ego*' [i.e. I (am) Arcadia too]. Although it is a standard *memento mori* on its own, the shepherd in the painting is clearly pointing at the ARC of ARCADIA. Could it not simply be that Poussin was indicating 'I am in Arques'? The very existence of an empty tomb— which it must be said looks more like a bunker than a tomb—must arouse our suspicions. So soon as Saunière had the documents decoded, it would have been apparent to those who knew of the treasure's whereabouts that he would look to Poussin's painting, rapidly take the hint and look for the tomb in the painting at Arques. They would therefore make it their business to buy him off and to remove the treasure to some safer place.

The ruins of the house of the shepherd, Ignace Paris, are still visible, perched on a hill near Rennes-les-Bains. In 1645, he came rushing into Rennes-le-Château, his hands filled with gold coins, which he claimed to have found in a cave at the bottom of a narrow ravine. But the villagers did not believe him, he would not take them back to his hoard, and he was hanged for theft.

Alternatively, of course, it may be that Saunière *did* investigate the tomb, found the Priory treasure and used it to his own ends.

We certainly have evidence that Poussin was privy—or believed himself to be so—to a great secret. A letter written to Nicolas Fouquet by his brother in 1656 tells us:

> He and I discussed certain things, which I shall with ease be able to explain to you in detail. Things which will give you through M. Poussin advantages which even kings would have great pains to draw from him, and which it is possible that nobody else will ever rediscover in the centuries to come. And, what is more, these are things so difficult to discover that nothing now on this earth can prove of better fortune nor be its equal.

Only a few years before in 1645, a shepherd named Ignace Paris had rushed excitedly into the village with his hands full of gold coins. He was at once interrogated by the villagers. He told them that, whilst searching for a lost sheep, he had climbed down a narrow ravine somewhere close to the village. The sheep had fled into a cave, in which, he said, he had found many chests full of gold and a number of human skeletons. The villagers disbelieved him and hanged him for theft.

Apparently his questioners had challenged Paris to show them this cave in proof of his story and he refused. That he refused to do so with a noose around his neck indicates either that he was a singularly stupid shepherd or that there was no such cave.

On Saunière's return from Paris, he continued his restoration—or maybe, by now, his investigation—of the church. He uncovered a stone slab depicting a man and a boy on the same horse—perhaps a representation of Sigisbert's flight (and thus, perhaps 'cheval de dieu', if one regards Sigisbert as a descendant of Christ). He also found three ancient skeletons and a pot full of jewels and coins. The Priory would have us believe that the skeletons are those of Sigisbert, his son and his grandson, that they were known as the Hermit Princes and hid in caves near Rennes-le-Château during the Moorish invasion.

He also effaced the inscriptions on the headstone and flagstone on the grave of the last of the d'Hautpouls. He was unaware that these had already been transcribed. The reason for this act of vandalism is that these inscriptions provided anagrams and keys for the texts in the ciphered documents.

He then took to making long journeys out of the village with a suitcase. Sometimes he was absent for as much as a week. At about this time too, money orders started to flood in from all over Europe, made out to Marie Desnarnaud, his housekeeper, friend and confidante.

Somehow, Saunière had become rich.

He completed the restoration of the church, and in 1900 bought land in order to build a new house, the Villa Bethania, and a private retreat, the Tour Magdala (the significance of the names is apparent) in which he kept his fine library. He redecorated the church in a gaudy, strangely pagan style. He created an orangery and a zoological garden. He gave huge parties for his parishioners and received such guests as the Archduke Johann von Habsburg, Emperor Franz-Josef's cousin.

In 1902 a new bishop of Carcassonne, Monseigneur de Beauséjour, was appointed. He thoroughly disapproved of Saunière and demanded an explanation of his wealth. They fought an increasingly bitter battle until, in 1915, Rome placed Saunière under an interdict on a charge of simony.

In 1903, too, Saunière fell out with his close friend, Abbé Henri Boudet, curé of nearby Rennes-les-Bains, who had taught him much of the history of the region and who had encouraged his work on the church. Suddenly too, Saunière was in financial difficulties and had to sell many of his precious possessions. Just before Boudet's death on 30 March 1915, Saunière was selling medals and rosaries to invalid soldiers.

On 26 March 1915, Boudet wrote to the bishop. He believed that he could throw some light, he said, on the death of Fr. Rescanière, another priest, whose body had been found on the morning of 1 February, after he had received a visit from two unknown people at one o'clock in the morning.

The bishop's delegate arrived at Boudet's house on 30 March, Boudet had already had two other visitors. They had murdered him. Nothing had been taken from the house. There is good

reason to suppose that Boudet had been Saunière's paymaster, acting, perhaps, as the authors of *The Holy Blood and the Holy Grail* suppose, as an intermediary between Saunière and the Priory of Sion.

Boudet remains a key figure in the mystery. The story of his having acquired some important secret at second hand from the Abbé Cauneille may well be true. Cauneille wrote two books said to be devoted to the mystery—*The Ray of Gold* and *The Line of Fire*: they are of the utmost rarity. He is himself said to have acquired the secret from Antoine Bigou, an eighteenth-century curé of Rennes-le-Château, commonly believed to have composed all the coded material over which Saunière laboured. Nowadays, many turn to Boudet's curious book, *La vraie langue celtique*, for hidden meanings and one of the local researchers on the mystery, Mme Tatiana Kletzky-Pradère, believes it is the central text. Without a doubt, the map and drawings of the area in Boudet's own hand which illustrate the book are worth closer examination.

In the last two years of his life, Saunière was restored to wealth and spent as lavishly as before. On 17 January 1917, he suffered a severe stroke and was found lying at the foot of the Tour Magdala. He lived for another five days. Before his death, he made his last confession to his friend Rivière, the curé of Esperaza. Whatever he revealed so shocked Rivière that for many months

One of the strange illustrations of rock formations from *La vraie langue celtique*. (Boudet signed his illustrations, *Edmond* Boudet.) Several modern editions of this work have appeared, including one with a preface by Pierre Plantard, whose grandfather was a friend of Saunière's.

he was an altered man. He refused Saunière the consolation of the last sacraments which can only indicate that, whatever his sins, the old priest was unrepentant to the last.

The Origins of Saunière's Wealth

There is plenty of evidence of Saunière's wealth, and although some of it may have come from contemporary sources (the Priory of Sion, the House of Habsburg and the Vatican have all been suggested), some of it was certainly of antique origin and most probably from a treasure hoard. He gave, for example, a beautiful and very ancient chalice to the priest Grassaud, and a considerable number of rare sixth- and seventh-century coins to the Abbé Courtauly, according to Gérard de Sède who states that he has seen them.

Other finds have been made in the area. A gold ingot weighing fifty kilos was found in a nearby field in 1860 and another weighing nearly twenty kilos, made up of Arab coins crudely melted down, was found in a wood. In 1928, a large gold statuette, partly melted down and only recognizable as such by its feet, was discovered in a ruined cottage close to the stream of Couleurs. A crucible with faint traces of gold in it was found in Montazels, where Saunière would go on his trips with his suitcase.

It seems then that Saunière found treasure at the same time as he discovered the secret, whatever it may be, of the Priory of Sion. Whether there is any treasure left today, what it might consist of and whether it is worth looking for, is another matter.

The most superficially plausible suggestion as to the hoard's contents was succinctly summarized by Henry Lincoln in an article based on the first BBC Chronicle programme on the subject, *The Lost Treasure of Jerusalem?* which was screened in 1972:

Romans and Visigoths had crossed paths elsewhere than here, and it is this crossing of paths that provides one of the most dramatic clues to the mystery. In A.D. 410 the Visigoths sacked Rome. The historian Procopius records the event, and describes the booty taken. He tells us that this included, '... the treasures of Solomon, the king of the Hebrews, a sight most worthy to be seen. For they were adorned for the most part with emeralds, and in the olden time they had been taken from Jerusalem by the Romans.'

This is a reference to the sacking of the Holy City by the Roman Emperor Titus in A.D. 70 and indeed Titus' Arch in Rome still shows the Temple Treasure with the great Menorah—the Seven-Branched Candlestick—clearly in evidence, as it was borne in the triumphal procession. This, then, is the treasure which Procopius tells us was snatched by the Visigoths, to become part of the booty from their many wars.

In the Fifth Century the Visigothic Kingdom straddled the Pyrenees. Their accumulated booty was well guarded. Part was used to finance the running of the State, and was held at Toulouse, their French capital. In A.D. 507 that 'state treasury' was captured by Clovis, king of the Franks. Some fifty miles away, however, at Carcassonne, was the more precious part of the Visigoths' Treasure. This was the 'ancient' or 'holy' treasure which—like the English crown jewels—was guarded as a symbol of the power, continuity and faith of the State. This, according to Procopius, was the treasure of which 'Solomon's' formed part. He relates how, after the capture of Toulouse, Clovis went on to besiege Carcassonne ... 'for he well knew that the Holy Treasure was there. That treasure which aforetimes Alaric the Elder had taken as booty when Rome fell to his hand.' But at Carcassonne the Visigoths held firm and eventually Clovis abandoned the siege.

Part of the Holy Treasure was later taken from Carcassonne to Toledo, the Spanish Capital of the Visigoths. In 711, the Arabian Moors attacked Toledo and the treasure was hidden away for safety. In the ensuing period of conflict and unrest it was lost and forgotten. In the nineteenth century at Guarrazar near Toledo, the lost treasure was unearthed. But neither in that hoard, nor in the detailed accounts of booty captured by the Arabs and the Franks, is there any trace of the Jerusalem Treasure. The last records place it in Carcassonne, a mere twenty miles from Aereda—Rennes-le-Château. Finally, under the assaults of their enemies, the Visigothic Empire dwindled to a tiny area known as the Razès—of which Aereda was a principal city, and one of the few remaining strongholds of their fading power. It would seem not unreasonable to suppose that it was also the repository of their remaining wealth. Could it have been the final resting-place of the Holy Treasure?

Following an interpretation of the designs in the church of Rennes-le-Château, Stanley James discovered this cave in May 1983 in the Bézis valley near Arques. Inside he found representations of a black hand print, a skull and crossbones, and a cross. Would-be investigators should note that the looseness of the soil and rock render it a potential death trap.

The trouble with this is that although Procopius records that the Visigoths took the treasure to France in A.D. 410, he also records in *De Bello Vandalico* Book II that Belisarius captured it in Carthage (where it had been taken from Rome in 455 by Genseric the Vandal king) and took it to Byzantium whence the Emperor Justinian 'straightway sent these treasures to the sanctuaries of the Christians in Jerusalem'. Furthermore, he records that after Clovis abandoned the siege of Carcassonne, the Visigothic general Ibbas, 'taking all the treasure which lay in the city of Carcassonne, marched swiftly back to Ravenna'.

To an age that could produce before the awestruck eyes of the multitude such 'relics' as the Spear of Longinus, the Cup and Knife used by our Lord at the Last Supper, and the Thirty Pieces of Silver, the existence of the vanished temple treasures of Jerusalem, including those that the Jews themselves admitted had been lost in the destruction of the First Temple, in two places at the same time, presented no great difficulty. During the dark and turbulent age following the break-up of the Roman Empire, the looted treasures of the warrior kings changed hands

Right: This map of the area to the east of Rennes-le-Château was prepared by the learned Henri Boudet for a seemingly absurd book, *La vraie langue celtique*, published in 1886. Many believe it contains clues to the whereabouts of treasure. Another book by Boudet, entitled *Lazare, veni foras* (i.e. 'Lazarus, come outside'), was burned by his bishop in the 1890s.

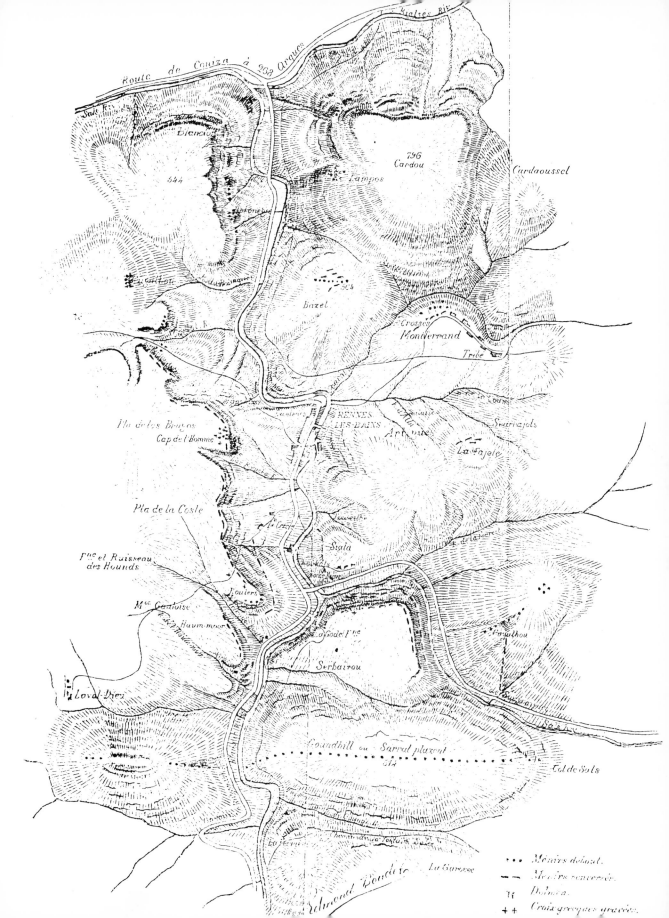

Route de Couiza à 968 Arques

Salz Riv

Dienne

544

796
Cardou

Cardaoussel

Lampos

504

Bazel

Crosses
Montferrand

Tribe

RENNES
LES-BAINS

Arbonne

Sarrajols

Pla de les Brugos
Cap de l'Homme

La Fajele

Pla de la Coste

Siala

F.ne et Ruisseau
des Hounds

Fouliers

M.on Couloise

F. de Haum-moor

La Crode F.ne

Serbairou

Paulhou

Lexal-Dieu

Grandhill ou Sarral plazent
514

Col de Sals

Berre

La Ferre

La Gavasse

Edmond Boudet

. . .   Menirs debout.
- - -   Menirs renversés.
 ‖   Dolmen.
+ +   Croix grecques gravées.

continuously. Any magnificent treasure associated by tradition with one or other of the sackings of Rome almost automatically became a part of the lost treasure of Jerusalem. Any suggestion as to the contents of the Rennes-le-Château hoard, therefore, is the wildest speculation. The only certainty is the undoubted arrival and dispersal of substantial Visigothic treasure in the region during the fifth and sixth centuries.

Whether there is any treasure left today, depends on whether Saunière was selling off a treasure hoard or was in the pay of some other agency. Since he signed a contract for eight million francs worth of new building work only a week before he died it may be reasonable to suppose that his original source of income had not been exhausted. The spokesman for the Priory of Sion, Pierre Plantard, claims that the hoard was indeed the lost treasure of Jerusalem, that it is now in the hands of the Priory and that they will eventually return it to Israel. However, given the nature of other pronouncements by the Priory it would be foolish to take this at face value.

Rennes-le-Château has become the province of those who love elaborate cryptography, arcane theories about the Dark Ages based on hypothesis rather than evidence, and recently, speculation that 'the core of the treasure is a strange artefact, an inexplicable power source created by some ancient, long-forgotten technology, or brought to Earth in a starship . . .'!

FURTHER ACTION

The chances of a newcomer genuinely interested in treasure finding any solution to the Priory's riddles are minimal. An example of how complex and overworked the attempts to decode them can become is Stanley James's *The Treasure Maps of Rennes-le-Château*. However, he draws one conclusion which may be worth investigation. He identified pointers to a site in the Bézis valley near Arques, between the hills of Berco Grande and Berco Petite and, in the exact spot where he expected to find something, there was a cave. Here he discovered strange markings in the rock that included representations of a black hand print, a skull and crossbones, and a cross.

A new line of enquiry based upon Visigothic and Merovingian settlement in the region and upon previous discoveries seems the most promising approach. As any metal detectorist, or 'coin shooter' knows, one of the golden rules of treasure hunting is to persevere at sites which have previously yielded finds. The large gold statuette found close to the stream of Couleurs, suggests one such site, although it was obviously transferred from nearby.

RHOSSILI BAY, GOWER PENINSULA, SOUTH WALES
THE DOLLAR SHIP

Rhossili Bay lies on the westernmost point of the Gower Peninsula in South Wales. It is a wild and, even now, sparsely populated stretch of coastline, renowned for its natural beauty. Unprotected from the wind and rain, large breakers pound the Sands, which stretch for nearly three miles; at the southern end lies Worms Head Point and at the northern, Bury Holms Island.

The area was notorious for the pirates and wreckers who operated there, but the most famous story of all is that of 'The Dollar Ship', a Spanish galleon that was shipwrecked during the seventeenth century somewhere on Rhossili Sands. Although the exact date is not known, it was probably between 1660 and 1690. Local tradition maintains that the ship contained Catherine of Braganza's dowry for her marriage to Charles II, although no details are known as to the galleon's name or its destination. What is certain, however, is that it contained a large number of Spanish silver coins. Some estimates put the figure as high as 400,000 coins.

The money lies scattered on the shore, hidden by the shifting sands and protected by the pounding surf and treacherous tides. An early story concerning the treasure tells of a man known as Mansell of Henllys who was supposed to have seized a large amount of the money and fled the country. Local legend maintains that the Spectral Chariot of Rhossili Sands, a black coach pulled by four black horses which is reputed to career along the beach, is his. Whether there is any truth in this is unimportant as he certainly did not get all the treasure.

The Appearance of the Coins

In 1807 William Bevan and a few other local men noticed that during an exceptional ebb-tide the sands had shifted in the vicinity of Diles Lake, about half-way along the bay. When they reached the spot they discovered a mass of coins. They

Catherine of Braganza was the Portuguese princess who married Charles II in 1662. Local tradition in the Gower Peninsula maintains that a galleon bearing Catherine of Braganza's dowry to Charles was wrecked in Rhossili Bay. An immense quantity of Spanish silver coins was briefly uncovered in 1807 by the action of the tide, and again in 1833.

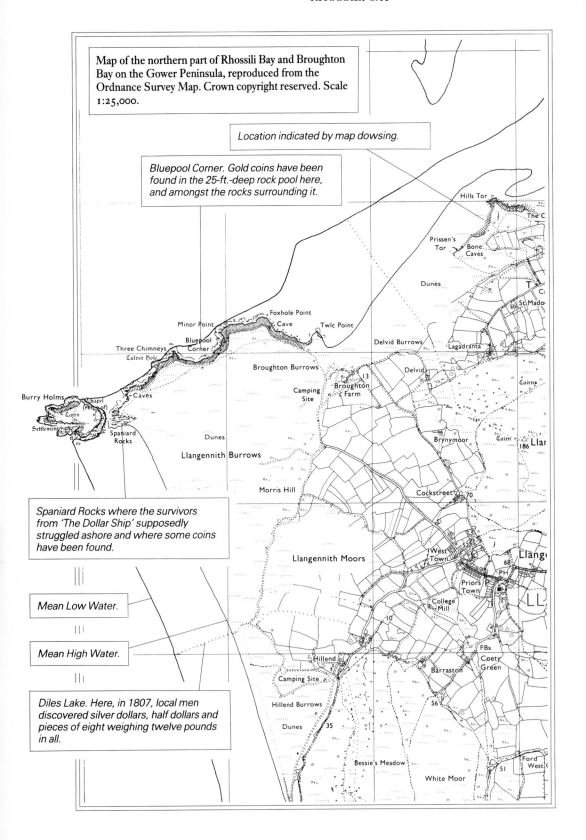

Map of the northern part of Rhossili Bay and Broughton Bay on the Gower Peninsula, reproduced from the Ordnance Survey Map. Crown copyright reserved. Scale 1:25,000.

Location indicated by map dowsing.

Bluepool Corner. Gold coins have been found in the 25-ft.-deep rock pool here, and amongst the rocks surrounding it.

Spaniard Rocks where the survivors from 'The Dollar Ship' supposedly struggled ashore and where some coins have been found.

Mean Low Water.

Mean High Water.

Diles Lake. Here, in 1807, local men discovered silver dollars, half dollars and pieces of eight weighing twelve pounds in all.

frantically tried to gather as many as they could before the tide turned and drove them back to the shore—William Bevan even took off his trousers, tied the ends of the legs together and used this to carry the coins. When they eventually had to give up they were in possession of silver dollars, half dollars and pieces of eight weighing twelve pounds. They had also found a cask of iron wire and some pewter.

The silver was not seen again for another twenty-five years or so. Then in 1833, after a fierce gale, four local men were lucky enough to be in the right place at the right time and found that the coins had been uncovered once more. The news of their find soon spread and a crowd of treasure-seekers flocked to the beach. The event has been likened to a mini gold rush and certainly quarrelling and fighting broke out as people staked their claims. Needless to say the tide soon made things very difficult. The coins were hidden by the sands again. The searchers tried to mark the spot with a cork buoy but it had been swept away when they returned. Again there is no doubt that they did not manage to collect all the coins. The men described how the water swept hundreds of silver dollars off their shovels as they struggled against the incoming tide. It was reported in the local paper, *The Cambrian*, that the local lord of the manor, C. R. M. Talbot Esquire, waived all claim to the silver. Many of the poorer members of the local community benefited enormously. This had also happened at the time of the earlier find in 1807.

The coins found were dated between 1625 and 1639, from the reign of Philip IV and were, according to some reports, Peruvian dollars minted in Potosi. Since then, no major discoveries have been reported although a few coins have been found in a group of rock pools known as Spaniard Rocks at the northern end of the Sands, so called because this is where the survivors from the shipwreck struggled ashore. The main reason for this lack of success is that the shoreline of the Bay has been greatly eroded during the last two centuries and the location of the wreck is now permanently under several feet of water. However, the coins must have been shifted by the strong tides during the ensuing years and if one could only work out where in this vast area of sand they have been deposited by the prevailing currents there may be up to 200,000 coins to be found.

Bluepool Corner

A less daunting prospect, perhaps, though no less tricky, is the treasure to be found in Bluepool Corner, a small cove round the point beyond Spaniards Rock. This contains a large rock pool, about 25 ft. deep, which lies at the foot of tall cliffs. The local people occasionally swim here and gold coins have been found amongst the rocks round the pool and in the pool itself. These coins are of a slightly later date than the ones from the 'Dollar Ship' but are also of Hispanic origin. Again it is the tide that has prevented more being found—as the cove can only be approached at low tide via Broughton Sands, and anyone still inside when the incoming tide has rounded Minor Point at the eastern corner of the cove, is trapped.

John Howland, who has provided much of the information for this account, hopes to overcome this difficulty by organizing a party of experienced rock climbers who would climb down the steep cliffs and then back up again as the tide came sweeping in. This would mean that they had the maximum amount of time to make a thorough search of the pool and surrounding area.

FURTHER ACTION

Winter and early spring are the best seasons to search for the coins on the Sands, with an all-motion discriminatory metal detector. At this time of year much of the sand will have been removed by the tides. However, the weather will not be very favourable on this unsheltered coast. In summer the beach, although not crowded, is fairly busy and so there will be a certain amount of litter. Another drawback for the detectorist is the vast area that lies uncovered at low tide. It might be possible to work out roughly where the coins have been deposited by the currents, from careful study of tidal charts, kept in the local records office, and Admiralty charts, although this would be a lengthy task. Do not be misled by the two wrecks that are visible at low tide—one is a

passenger ship that sank 160 years ago and the other, below Rhossili Cliffs, is the remains of a ship that was carrying a cargo of timber.

If you are interested in Bluepool Corner, John Howland can be contacted through *The Searcher* Magazine, Token Publishing Ltd, Crossways Road, Grayshott, Hindhead, Surrey, UK.

The Gower Coast by George Edmunds is probably the most useful and reliable guide to the area.

Rhossili Sands. As well as the discoveries of 1807 and 1833, a number of small finds have been made in the pools of Spaniard Rocks and at Bluepool Corner, a small cove to the north.

SAN SABA MINE, MENARD, TEXAS, USA

LOST SILVER MINE

The story of the mines of San Saba is a curious mixture of fact, fiction, speculation and downright lies. We have no reputable authority for its existence, and the only reason for its inclusion in this book is the sheer resilience of the legend. The San Saba story will not lie down and die.

The San Saba river flows into the River Colorado, north-west of Austin in Texas. It was discovered by the Spanish in 1732 in the course of a military campaign deep into the lands of the Eastern Apaches. The Spaniards, who had hitherto colonized the south and the west, had long intended to annexe the San Saba region. As early as 1725, Francisco Hidalgo, a Franciscan priest, had put forward a plan to Christianize the Lipans, a branch of the Eastern Apaches.

The Lieutenant-General's Story

Our first authority—and probably the source of the story—is Don Bernardo de Miranda, Lieutenant-General of Texas. In 1756, he rode out of San Fernando (now San Antonio) with a small company to make an exploratory survey of the Lipans' territory. In the Llano region, near Honey Creek, his party discovered a hill rich in silver, which they named Cerro del Almagre. Miranda wrote an ecstatic report: 'the mines which are in the Cerro del Almagre are so numerous that I guarantee to give to every settler in the province of Texas a full claim ...' He went on to state that he had heard from Apaches of rich silver deposits north of Llano Estacado, in Commanche territory, six days ride away, but he could not, or dared not investigate.

He brought ore samples back to San Fernando three weeks later and instantly filed a recommendation that the Spaniards should establish a *presidio* or fortress, in the region. Despite the richness of the samples, the authorities hesitated. Perhaps they wished to gauge popular reaction to Miranda's tale. Perhaps their suspicions, like ours, were aroused by so opportune a find, and Miranda was either telling the truth or engaged in a little private expansionism.

After twenty months more, they called Miranda's bluff, if bluff it was, just as Elizabeth I called Ralegh's. Miranda would mount an expedition at his own expense. If he brought back thirty mule-loads of ore samples to Camp Mazapil (a full 700 miles from Cerro del Almagre) and if on assay they proved as rich as the first samples, the authorities would consider building a *presidio* and giving him its command.

Miranda set off again in November 1757 and was never heard of again.

San Saba

Although Miranda's fate is not known his story lived on. A Spanish *presidio* had been established at San Luis de las Amarillas, north of the San Saba river, and about eighty-five miles north-west of Cerro del Almagre. Its first commander, Captain Diego Ortiz de Parrilla sought permission to move his garrison to the Llano region of the river before the presidio had even been completed. His request was refused.

Parrilla was obviously familiar with Miranda's survey. He repeated his request in 1758 and mentioned the need for protection of the work on some rich veins of silver 'which, it is claimed, have

SAN SABA MINE

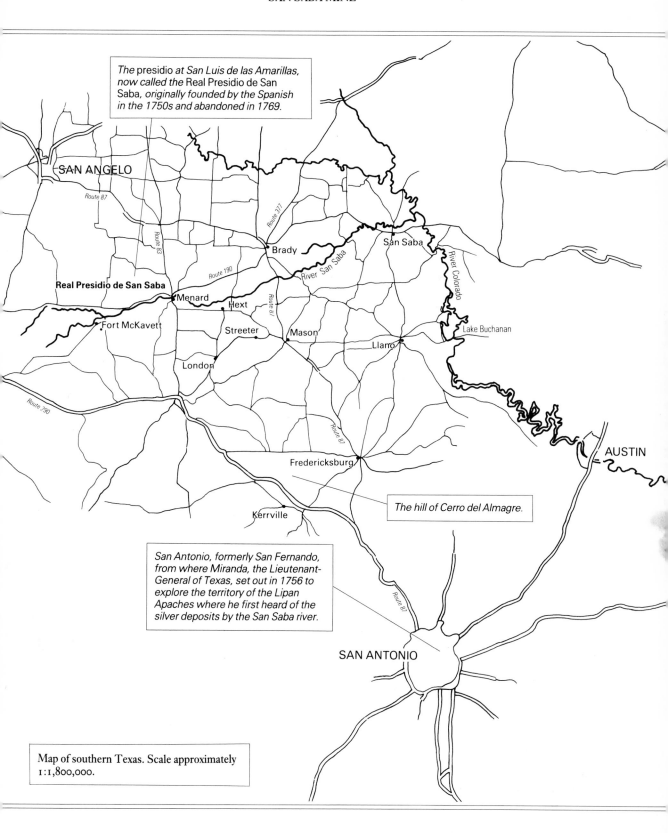

The presidio at *San Luis de las Amarillas, now called the* Real Presidio de San Saba, *originally founded by the Spanish in the 1750s and abandoned in 1769.*

The hill of *Cerro del Almagre.*

San Antonio, formerly San Fernando, from where Miranda, the Lieutenant-General of Texas, set out in 1756 to explore the territory of the Lipan Apaches where he first heard of the silver deposits by the San Saba river.

Map of southern Texas. Scale approximately 1:1,800,000.

been discovered ...'. Again, the authorities refused his request. At sunrise on 16 March 1758, a mission just three miles away downriver had been attacked by a force of 2,000 Comanches, who massacred most of the priests and razed the building to the ground.

Constantly undermanned and under threat from the Indians, Parrilla's *presidio* stood for another twelve years. It was the largest fortress in Texas but had little apparent justification for its existence. The Marques de Rubi, Charles III's Inspector-General, visited in 1766: 'It affords as much protection to the interests of His Majesty in New Spain as a ship anchored in mid-Atlantic would afford in preventing foreign trade with America.' Three years later, the Spanish abandoned it.

A Lieutenant Juan Padilla visited both Cerro del Almagre and San Saba in 1810. The author of the report on this expedition, José Maria Garcia, expounded on the rich ore to be found. More impressively, Ignacio Obregon, the inspector of mines, collected impressive samples of ore in 1812 and recommended the *presidio*'s reoccup-ation. The Mexican revolution and the expulsion of the Spanish prevented either recommen-dation from being acted upon.

Both these reports contributed largely to the legend of treasure, though neither specified where this mineral wealth was to be found.

Jim Bowie's Expedition

In 1829, Jim Bowie the slave-dealer, pioneer-scout and land speculator who was to die gloriously on the ramparts of the Alamo, learned that the Lipans of the Llano region came to San Antonio once or twice a year to barter silver. It had thus far proved impossible to learn the source of this silver. The Indians were sworn to secrecy under threat of death.

Deviously, Bowie cultivated the tribe's trust and friendship. He presented a silver-plated rifle to Xolic, their chief, in blatant contravention of the law and, following a meeting at San Pedro Springs, was adopted into the tribe. After some months, he claimed, his nominal brethren showed him what he had come for. He did not specify whether this was a quantity of silver bullion or a rich vein of silver. At the nearest opportunity, he deserted them, fled to San Antonio and prepared to return with a small but heavily armed force.

Another account of this story is given by a friend, Cephas K. Ham. Ham claims that it was Jim's brother, Rezin P. Bowie, who saw the source of the silver. 'It was not far from the fort. The shaft was about eight feet deep.' Ham also says that it was he, not Jim Bowie, who was adopted by the Indians—Comanches, not Lipans—and came close to being shown the mine.

Whatever the case, Bowie's treacherous 1831 party was eleven strong and included his brother Rezin and Ham. They left San Antonio on 2 November and were still one day short of their destination—a mere 150 miles away—after twenty days. It is to be presumed that they stopped somewhere en route. Perhaps, less certain than they claimed of wealth at the end of their journey, they made a detour to Cerro del Almagre along the way.

On 21 November, they camped in an oak grove on a point of land framed by a creek's sharp curve.

Jim Bowie, famous for the Bowie knife and for his death in defence of the Alamo, is said to have been shown a quantity of silver near the San Saba river by Lipan Indians in 1829. In 1831, he returned with a well-armed band but was driven off by a large Indian war party. The 'Bowie Mine' has been hunted for ever since.

The Apaches proved to be amongst the most intractable of the Indian tribes for white settlers. At Tayopa and Superstition Mountain, as well as San Saba, their often ferocious resistance to the newcomers spelt great trouble.

At daylight, 164 Indians attacked. The fight lasted the whole day. When at last the Indians drew back, 50 braves were left dead about the camp and a further 35 lay wounded. The Texans had made the most of their cover and their superior firepower. They had lost just one man and three of their number were wounded. This effectively constituted the end of the expedition.

It was eighteen days before Bowie and his rabble struggled back into San Antonio. Ham relates that Bowie returned to San Luis with thirty men some time not long afterwards. This time, he

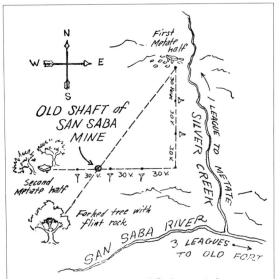

'Carlota's Chart.' A girl named Carlota copied some documents in the Spanish archives of Monclova, Mexico in the 1850s and fed out part of the information to her associates. This led them to Silver Creek, north-west of the old Spanish fortress by the San Saba River, where Carlota said they would find a stash of 2,000 silver bars. The chart contains the information she gave them.

The ruins of the *presidio* have afforded little joy to treasure-seekers. A smelter and eleven silver bullets have been found to suggest that there was ever mineral wealth in the immediate area. The smelter is thought to have been Parrilla's. There are, of course, the inevitable traditions, with which the reader will by now be familiar. A gold and silver bell was cast within sight of the mission and lies buried in the river-bed. A lake close by was artificially created by the Spaniards to conceal their riches. A clear trail once led north-west from the fortress to Silver Creek, also called Silver Mine. These traditions are characteristic of Latin American treasure stories, notably that of the bells, perhaps because the Indians knew nothing of the casting of metals before the Spaniards' arrival and associated the rare and sonorous metal in the church tower with the precious minerals within.

There are other stories which ring truer. A Lipan led some Austin citizens to 'an old Spanish mine' in 1842 or thereabouts, and a former captive of the Comanches was about to show Captain Billingsley 'the Bowie mine' when the Indians caught and killed the bearer of the secret. These are vague stories, but others, like Grumble's story, are more precise.

reached his destination but could not find his secret shaft. The legend of the San Saba treasure, by association with Bowie, was now firmly established as part of American folklore. There was no shortage of 'authorities' to compound and confuse the legend further.

In 1828, for example, Elias Wightman, a surveyor in Texas, included the approximate location of the San Saba mine upon a map which he prepared, and about the same time portrayed it in glowing colours. Captain Marryat, the English novelist, wrote in 1843, 'The Comanches have a great profusion of gold, which they obtain from the neighbourhood of the San Seba (*sic*) hills, and work it themselves into bracelets, armlets, diadems ...' This not only conflicts with what we know of the Indians, but marks a further stage in the development of the story. The philosopher's stone of romance has turned rumoured silver into gold. One Dr Roemer, a German visitor to the *presidio* in 1847, recorded 'a persistent rumour among the Texas settlers that the Spaniards had worked some silver mines in the vicinity of the fort'.

Grumble the Rancher

Grumble was a rancher in the San Saba area when, in 1857, he heard of a Mexican woman in San Antonio who had once helped the Comanches to gather silver ore. He sought this woman out, and she spoke openly of her experience, but emphasized that she had never visited the Indians' mine itself.

She claimed that the Comanches used to camp in the deserted *presidio*, cross the San Saba and travel south for about two miles, following Los Moros Creek. Then the Indian males would leave the others at a fixed point and return, sometimes as little as an hour later, bearing the silver. She believed that the halt was about half a mile from the mine. Grumble asked to be taken to the halt. She consented. Their rendezvous was never kept. Grumble was shot dead in a bar-room duel. The woman, who was afraid of the Comanches, refused to take any other speculator to the site.

Aurelio Gondora's Treasure Maps

Aurelio Gondora was a shy young Spaniard who became the tutor of a man named Merchant in 1896. As a consequence of an argument, Gondora showed Merchant the treasure maps of Texas, Oklahoma and New Mexico which his father had bequeathed to him.

Gondora had been told that, shortly before they abandoned the *presidio* in 1769, the Spaniards had all their horses stolen by Comanches, rendering all the mines save one—the main mine—inaccessible. This mine was close to the junction of a creek and the San Saba. It lay to the east of the *presidio*, where the Spaniards had a small fortification.

Merchant saw the map just once, and Gondora was later stabbed to death and his trunk containing the maps stolen. Merchant happened, however, to visit one of the sites indicated on the maps and found something unspecified. He at once became a firm believer in Gondora's maps. He went in search of the San Saba site and, on the basis of certain ruins which he presumably took to be the fortifications of which Gondora had spoken, he identified Calf Creek as the one on the map. He never however found the mine.

FURTHER ACTION

The area of search for the San Saba treasure is necessarily very extensive. There are a large number of possible sites and it cannot be claimed that legend or finds give us reason to support the claims of any one.

Silver Creek, however, seems our best starting point. In 1858 a girl named Carlota, who worked in the Spanish archives in Monclova, in Mexico, produced an old *derrotero* (since lost). This sent a man named Dixon to the creek where, it is said, there was a storehouse of 2,000 silver bars, allegedly derived from fourteen Spanish mines. Dixon and his associates were told to dig 60 ft. down, but soon gave up. They claimed that there were signs that someone else had dug there before them. Later, a man called Longworth dug the full 60 ft. but encountered an underground lake beneath the limestone. He was never able to pump the water out of his shaft. Metal detectors have given positive responses at this spot. Great sub-aqua expertise will be needed if it is to be explored further through Dixon's shaft.

The remains of the presidio are now to be found about a mile from the modern town of Menard, which is to the north-west of Austin, Texas, on the road from Junction to Eden. The mission, two miles south of Menard, is no longer visible, its stones having been pushed into the San Saba river in the course of some field clearance. A clear trail once led north-west from the presidio to Silver Creek.

It should be noted that the modern town of San Saba has nothing to do with our story.

SUPERSTITION MOUNTAIN, PHOENIX, ARIZONA, USA

MIGUEL PERALTA'S LOST VEIN AND 'THE OLD DUTCHMAN'

Gold fever still runs high in Apache Junction, Arizona. Old prospectors offer the tourist genuine treasure maps stained by age and coffee, they only want a few dollars in exchange. They would have used the maps themselves, of course, if the rough terrain of Superstition Mountain were not so hard on old bones, and they just happened to see you and liked the look of your face. They tell tales of rich veins of gold glimpsed one night in a lightning flash, of nuggets found and lost, of Apache savagery and, of course, of the Old Dutchman.

And up on the mountain itself, there will be a handful of people at any time with picks and packs and maps handed down to them, scouring the countless cliffs, canyons and ravines for the great mother lode. Some will give up after only a few days, scared off by a rattler or daunted by the perilous conditions. Others build cabins, sink shafts and stay for years.

It is not just the gold which lures people to Superstition Mountain. It is also the fascination of violent death. There are bigger mountains, and harder to climb, but none has claimed more lives or seen more torture. Even in the last fifty years, treasure-hunters have been found dead, some decapitated. Once they blamed the Apaches or more luridly the Apache Thunder God whose home it is, but more often men shot one another for the sake of claims or maps or even, as, for example, in the case of Benjamin Ferreira in April 1959, because his partner had found one of the many veins of fool's gold. Ferreira wanted it all to himself.

So famous has Superstition become as a place of murder that psychopaths like Herbert LeRoy Stockley have gone there looking for someone to kill. Stockley found a construction worker and his wife enjoying a treasure-hunting holiday and cut their throats.

Sierra de la Espuma

Superstition Mountain is not a mountain. It is a vast volcanic range of cliffs and peaks some thirty-five miles east of Phoenix. They have exotic names such as Geronimo's Head, Fish Creek, Picacho Butte, the Tortilla, Miner's Needle and Bluff Springs. They are commonly referred to as Superstition Mountain simply because, from the south-west, one enormous sheer façade is all that can be seen.

Francisco Vasquez de Coronado, coming north from Mexico in 1540 in search of one of the legendary Seven Golden Cities of Cibola, was probably the first European to set eyes on the mountain. The Indians told him that this was the home of their thunder god, where much gold could be found.

He and his little band of explorers rapidly discovered how difficult and dangerous it is to explore this jagged, unpredictable terrain. The Indians, for fear of their god, offered them no assistance. Several of the Spaniards are said to have died as they searched in vain for a route through the stormy sea of grey pumice which they knew as the *Sierra de la Espuma*, or 'Range of Foam'; their bodies, found later by their companions, were headless.

The survivors, unsurprisingly, had soon had enough of this dangerous diversion. Coronado christened the range *Monte Supersticion* and

The inhospitable range of cliffs and peaks to the east of Phoenix, Arizona, known as Superstition Mountain, has been the scene of high drama many times within the last 150 years. Weaver's Needle, visible in the foreground, is a recurring landmark in the stories.

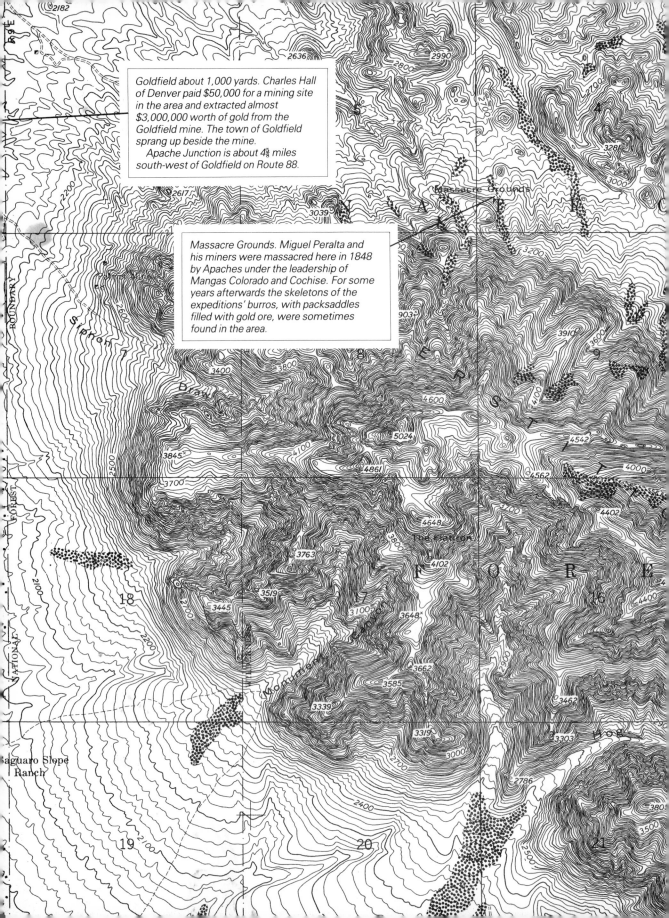

Goldfield about 1,000 yards. Charles Hall
of Denver paid $50,000 for a mining site
in the area and extracted almost
$3,000,000 worth of gold from the
Goldfield mine. The town of Goldfield
sprang up beside the mine.
    Apache Junction is about 4⅝ miles
south-west of Goldfield on Route 88.

Massacre Grounds. Miguel Peralta and
his miners were massacred here in 1848
by Apaches under the leadership of
Mangas Colorado and Cochise. For some
years afterwards the skeletons of the
expeditions' burros, with packsaddles
filled with gold ore, were sometimes
found in the area.

West Boulder Canyon, where Adolph Ruth's skull was found in 1931. Ruth believed he had instructions describing the whereabouts of Miguel Peralta's mine.

Map of the western half of Superstition Mountain, from the USGS Quadrangle, Arizona. Scale 1:24,000.

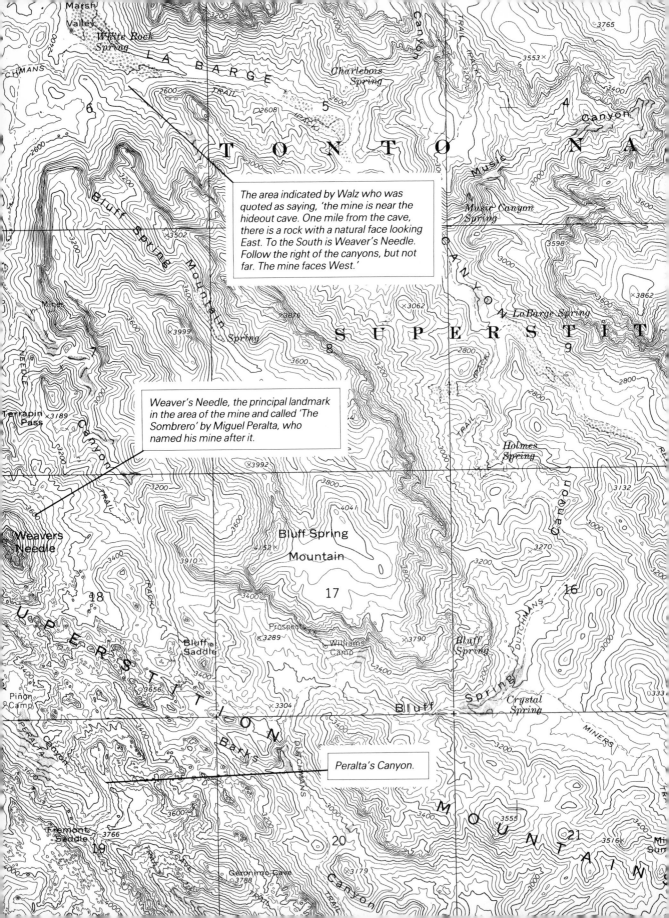

The area indicated by Walz who was quoted as saying, 'the mine is near the hideout cave. One mile from the cave, there is a rock with a natural face looking East. To the South is Weaver's Needle. Follow the right of the canyons, but not far. The mine faces West.'

Weaver's Needle, the principal landmark in the area of the mine and called 'The Sombrero' by Miguel Peralta, who named his mine after it.

Peralta's Canyon.

Map of the eastern half of Superstition Mountain, from the USGS Weaver's Needle Quadrangle, Arizona. Scale 1:24,000.

headed on northward to discover, soon afterwards, the Grand Canyon.

Miguel Peralta's Mine

The 'mountain's' new name and the legendary savagery of the Apaches in defence of their sacred grounds seem to have deterred further speculators for a further two and a half centuries.

In 1608 one Pedro Peralta de Cordoba was appointed Governor of Santa Fe (now in New Mexico). In 1776 his descendants were granted the title Baron de Colorado and a large area of land that included the *Sierra de la Espuma*. The Peralta family did not explore as far north as the *Sierra* until the early part of the nineteenth century when their silver mines became exhausted.

In 1845 Miguel Peralta came to Superstition and found a rich vein of almost pure gold on or near the mountain. To help himself memorize the site of the find before returning to Mexico to obtain men and equipment, he marked it in relation to the mountain's outstanding feature, a peculiar peak which, he said, resembled a sombrero. He would call his mine *Sombrero* after this peak. Known to the Mexican labourers as 'the finger of God' and to subsequent generations of explorers as Weaver's Needle, this landmark was to prove crucial in many of the future searches for the mine. For three years after his return from Mexico, Peralta and his workforce of several hundred peons extracted millions of pesos' worth of pure gold concentrate from the Sombrero mine and shipped it back to Sonora. The Apaches, however, were just biding their time. Not only had these foreigners defiled sacred ground, but Apache girls are said to have been visiting some of the miners in camp. In 1848, Mangas Colorado brought a large force of braves from their stronghold in the Chiricahua Mountains and joined forces with the great Cochise to drive the sacrilegious interlopers from their land.

Peralta discovered their plans in time. He withdrew from the mine with all his men and livestock to a well-protected camp higher up the mountain. Traces of this camp, where they had kept the smelters to separate gold from the ore, are still to be seen. Some versions of the story

Chiricahua Apache. In a joint attack with Cochise, the Chiricahua Apaches massacred Miguel Peralta and his Mexicans at the site now known as Massacre Ground, on Superstition Mountain. Many *burro* skeletons were formerly found in the neighbourhood, their rotting packsaddles heavy with gold concentrate from Peralta's mine.

claim that Peralta buried a certain amount of gold near the mine, marking the spot with stones and making a sketch-map, which has never been found.

Once established in this temporary refuge, Peralta loaded the animals with all the gold already extracted and awaiting shipment. He also ordered that the entrance to the mine should be covered over and that all traces of mining activity should be swept away. He intended, presumably, to return one day when the dust had settled.

One of Peralta's peons, however, presumably lovesick and anxious to enjoy one last assignation with his Apache girl before leaving for Mexico, was captured with her that night. He revealed Peralta's plans. When the Mexicans moved out before dawn the next day, their enemies were already lying in wait for them.

The trap was sprung at the foot of the sheer cliffs at the north-west end of the mountain. Peralta and his armed guard were killed as arrows hailed down into the line. The pack animals bolted. The peons, who were not customarily equipped with weapons, were hacked down with stone hatchets. The party was slaughtered to a man. The site of the ambush is now known as Massacre Ground. US army troops discovered some bodies of the victims—although not Peralta's—in 1850.

For once, therefore, we have an accredited case of an unquestionable treasure of whose whereabouts the only witnesses are proven dead. The massacre also served to create a second treasure—the gold concentrate in the saddles of the pack animals. The burros fled into the many ravines and washes about the scene of the massacre. The Apaches did not pursue them. They attached no value to the unrefined gold that they carried. Even when, in the ensuing days, the Indians caught and killed some of the animals for food, they removed the saddlebags from the carcasses and left them behind. Others of the burros wandered farther afield and died with the packs still on their backs.

In the early 1850s, two prospectors, Hurley and O'Connor, found a dead burro with a full packsaddle. They must have known the story of the massacre of Peralta and his men, and quietly began a search for more in the same area. In the following weeks, they found another burro

Arizona. Gold prospectors in the last century.

skeleton and two more packsaddles. They were wiser than most of the fortunate treasure-hunters on Superstition. They pounded the concentrate and panned out the gold on the spot. They did not return to Apache Junction, where the slightest sign of excitement might have earned them a bullet. They simply packed up like any other disappointed prospectors and headed for the US mint in San Francisco. The gold fetched $37,000.

They returned over many years and increased their wealth with each visit. Inevitably, sharp-eyed and envious locals became suspicious. Their success rate had declined, and the danger—from outlaws and Apaches—had risen. Again, Hurley and O'Connor showed wisdom. They counted their blessings and their by now sizeable fortunes and gratefully retired. They died old and rich. The last packsaddle was found in 1914 by C. H. Silverlocke. The general area in which the packsaddles were found is now known as Goldfield.

The Old Dutchman

The most famous figure associated with Superstition Mountain enters the story in the mid-1860s. Although widely known as 'The Old Dutchman', Jakob Walz (originally, von Walzer) was in fact a German. Blessed—or cursed—with the eternal optimism of the compulsive gambler or prospector, he had been educated as a mining engineer at Heidelberg and had sought mineral wealth in Prussia and in Australia before taking ship for California and the great gold rush in 1848.

He had enjoyed no great success in California or in Arizona until, when working as an ordinary miner, he fell in love with a beautiful Apache girl named Ken-tee. She helped him to smuggle gold out of the extraordinarily rich mine at which he was employed. Eventually Walz was dismissed, although the case against him could not be proved.

Walz, then, nearing sixty but still a big, physically powerful man, now lived with Ken-tee in a small community a few miles from Superstition Mountain. One day they vanished. They returned several weeks later with two heavily laden burros. As soon as Walz began to make arrangements to dispatch gold to the mint at San Francisco, the secret was out. Walz had struck lucky. It was generally believed that he too must have found one of the lost packsaddles.

The Apaches, however, seem to have thought that Ken-tee must have betrayed the site of the mine, a closely guarded Indian secret. They raided Walz's home a few days later, seized Ken-tee and bore her off. Her neighbours pursued the raiding-party and rescued her from their clutches, but not before the braves had cut out her tongue. She died in Walz's arms within the hour.

Walz moved to Phoenix where he became known as an embittered, hard-drinking recluse. He brawled a lot and, as the truth about his find became known, he became famous. People came from great distances to see 'The Old Dutchman', the man who held the secret of a great fortune but could not be bothered to claim it. Wherever he went, he was followed. He led his avaricious pursuers from bar-room to bar-room, but never to his mine.

Three years after Ken-tee's death, however, another German arrived in Phoenix. It seems probable that Walz had sent for him. A carpenter by trade, Jacob Weiser, or Wisner, was an extrovert as Walz was an introvert. He became a popular and familiar figure in Phoenix until one day, he and Walz quietly vanished. They returned inside a month with sacks full of gold concentrate, consigned it to Wells Fargo for dispatch to the mint, and once more set off for Superstition Mountain.

There, they collected more gold and turned again for Phoenix. The Apaches attacked as they slept in an overnight camp. Walz escaped wearing only his shirt, shoes and stockings. He tore the shirt into strips and tied them round his feet so that he could run over the rough rocks. Weiser was fatally wounded by an arrow which plunged through his left arm and into his chest. He struggled to the home of Dr John D. Walker, one of Walz's few friends and died the following morning.

Walz returned to the 'mountain' from time to time after this setback, but more rarely as the years went by. His legend was now known throughout America and many people would have given anything to know his secret. Only a clever and ruthless man could have thwarted such an army of eager pursuers as Walz had now acquired. He was both. No charge of murder was ever proved against him, but it was generally thought unwise to stick too close on his trail. It is said, for example, that Walz and Weiser summarily killed two Mexicans whom they found poaching on their site. Between 1879 and 1885, Walz received a total of $254,000 from the mint.

It may be that one or two other searchers found Walz's mine during this period. A prospector named Joe Deering averred that he had gone through a hole which led him to it. He intended to share his knowledge with his listeners, but died in an accident before he could show them the way.

In 1880, two young men, thought to have been ex-soldiers, showed up at the little town of Pinal, their saddlebags filled with exceptionally pure gold. They claimed to have found a funnel-shaped opening in the rocks which led to a rich seam from which they could break off as much gold-bearing rock as they could carry. The opening, they said, was near a sharp pinnacle of rock.

Encouraged to return, they set off on the twenty-five-mile ride to Superstition, unaware that this was the last journey that they were to make. A rescue party found their naked bodies ten days later. Although the manner of their deaths bore some of the hallmarks of an Apache killing, popular opinion was that this was merely a ruse and that an interested townsman was responsible. Some suspected Walz, others a local trader who grew suddenly and unaccountably rich.

Walz's Legacy

Walz made his last journey to the mountain in 1890. He withdrew $15,000 worth of gold from a cache, not the mine. This was to be his legacy. In October of the following year, this pathetic, Faustian figure who had unwittingly exchanged happiness for enormous wealth, died at the house of a kind-hearted black woman named Julia Thomas. Walz left the $15,000 and directions to the mine to his friends. One of these, Dick Holmes, relates that Walz also confessed on his deathbed to the murder of his nephew, Julius, who had been invited over from Germany to share

the secret many years before and had talked too freely.

Walz's directions to the mine tantalize, but ultimately obfuscate more than they reveal. They certainly brought nothing but misfortune to those, like Julia Thomas, who spent the rest of their lives and fortunes in the fruitless search. The mine, he said, was in country 'so rough that you could be right in the mine without seeing it'. It was shaped like a funnel with the broad end uppermost. Shelves had been cut along the walls to help the miners to bring their loads up from the bottom. Peralta had also cut a tunnel through the hillside to the bottom of the shaft in order to simplify removal further. The mine contained an eighteen inch vein of rose quartz which was rich in gold nuggets and another vein of hematite quartz which was roughly one-third gold. Robert Petrasch, who helped Julia Thomas in her long search quotes Walz as follows: 'The mine is near the hideout cave. One mile from the cave, there is a rock with a natural face looking East. To the South is Weaver's Needle. Follow the right of the canyons, but not far. The mine faces West.'

The only problem with this is that Walz failed to identify the hideout cave, and one mile is indeed 'not far' in so enormous an area as that North of Weaver's Needle. Walz continued: 'The mine can be found at the spot on which the shadow of the tip of Weaver's Needle rests at exactly four in the afternoon.' During the course of a year, the shadow of the tip of Weaver's Needle falls on many places at four o'clock. To this day, the tourists gather to chase it. None has found more than a shadow.

Julia Thomas may have had some further clues, but they helped her no more than these two. She died in abject poverty after years of hunting. She passed on her information to Jim Bark, an Arizona rancher. He searched for a further fifteen years but found nothing.

They clearly believed that Walz had told the truth, even if that truth was insufficient. Whether their credulity was founded upon their knowledge of Walz's character or upon optimistic avarice, it is impossible to say. Whilst it is clear that Walz was a misanthrope and that he enjoyed his celebrity, it seems incredible that he can have been so irredeemably malignant as to take his secret to the grave whilst feeding to his only friends misleading information which could only and inevitably bring them misery. Locals have suggested that he used his knowlege to exploit Julia Thomas when, in the last days of his life, he needed a soft bed, regular meals and a woman's sympathy, but that he never had any intention of revealing the truth to her or to any of the other greedy hangers-on whom he despised. One of the many superstitions surrounding Superstition Mountain is that you can hear the Old Dutchman's laughter in the thunder as it echoes in the canyons.

The Voice of the Thunder God

While Jim Bark was following the shadow of the tip of Weaver's Needle, a new clue sent adventurers scurrying in another direction. An amateur prospector related a typically confused tale. It seemed that, before setting out on his last trip to the mine, Weiser had let slip to a grocer friend the fact that the shaft was just a little to the West of Massacre Ground and that it was marked by a huge boulder. There was indeed a huge boulder on the top of a hill to the West of Massacre Ground. Among the many eager treasure-seekers who came to look on it was Charles Hall of Denver. When the claims on the site came up for sale, Hall bought them for the apparently absurd sum of $50,000.

There was however some method in Hall's madness. As an experienced prospector, he had at once noticed distinct evidence that gold ore had been transported over the hill. He also recognized that the boulder was unlike anything else in that part of the country. He therefore reasoned that the diggings must have been somewhere on the top of the hill, since there could have been no point in bearing the gold upwards from a mine lower down, and that the boulder must have been brought there specially, presumably as a marker, by someone with many men at his command; probably Peralta.

Hall brought in the latest equipment, hired some men and sank a shaft at the very top of the hill. Nearly three million dollars' worth of gold were drawn from this 'Goldfield' mine over the next few years, and a wild town, also called Goldfield, complete with cathouses, gambling hells, saloons and all the other inevitable parasitic growths, grew up on the site.

The Apaches remained quiet at this large-scale invasion of their Thunder God's home. Then, one night the God spoke for himself. A huge thunderstorm shook the mountain. The worst rain in living memory streamed from the sky. At the north-west end of the mountain, the god's particular shrine, several distinct cascades were seen hurtling down the crags to form one great rushing torrent. Another such torrent swept over the mine. It buried everything under thousands of tons of rocks and sand.

The miners soon drifted away. Hall died. Only one man had the temerity to try to work the mine again. George Young, ex-mayor of Phoenix, bought the claim from Hall's daughters and speculated heavily, bringing in expensive new machinery and a workforce still larger than Hall's. The mother lode had been shifted by the flood. He sank a shaft in search of it and hit an underground river at 1,100 ft. Such was the pressure that the water level shot up to within 100 ft. of the surface, and there it still remains. Many efforts were made, but no one has succeeded in lowering the level by an inch.

Veni, Vidi, Vici

Of the many twentieth-century searchers, Adolph Ruth is notable, if only for the manner of his death. An elderly man, Ruth came from Washington in 1931 bearing a map which he believed to have emanated from the Peralta family. He set off into the mountain and disappeared. Six months later, a team of investigators found his skull close to the floor of West Boulder Canyon, where his guides had left him encamped on the first day. Two bullets had been shot through his brain. His body and possessions turned up a month later a considerable distance away.

Thus far, then, this appeared to be a standard Superstition Mountain murder, including an Apache-style decapitation. It is unlikely that Indians were responsible, however. No map was found amongst his possessions, and the motive was therefore almost certainly the theft of this precious, if fraudulent document. It was a little

Adolph Ruth tried his luck in Superstition Mountain in 1931 with a map said to be derived from the Peraltas. He was murdered shortly after setting off and his skull was found six months afterwards. The discovery, a month later, of a little notebook, the last of whose entries read: '*Veni, vidi, vici*' ('I came, I saw, I conquered'), made front page news.

book in Ruth's jacket pocket which was to make him briefly famous. He had copied his instructions into this book. These indicated a circle of not more than five miles diameter and centred on Weaver's Needle as the search area and continued:

> 'The first gorge on the south side from the west end of the range—they found a blazed trail which led them northward over a high ridge and then downward into a long canyon running North, and finally to a tributary canyon very deep, rocky and densely covered with a continuous thicket of scrub oak ... about two hundred feet across from a cave.'

Much lower down he had written Caesar's triumphant words, '*Veni, Vidi, Vici*'. Of all the last words that he could have chosen, none could have excited more public interest and enthusiasm. Superstition was front page news again, and the flow of prospectors redoubled.

The likelihood that Ruth actually found gold is very small. He was old and frail and could not have covered much rough terrain in a day. We know that he only pitched one camp and probably died within his first forty-eight hours on the mountain. It seems more likely that he had copied

out the famous words in anticipation of carving them on some rock, or that he had stumbled on that vein of fool's gold which was to cause Ferreira to kill in 1959.

Shortly after the Second World War, a mining engineer named Alfred Strong Lewis was prospecting on the Goldfield mining property when various little signs at the base of a large boulder caught his eye. He toppled the boulder over with dynamite and discovered an ancient mining shaft beneath. This was about a mile from the Massacre Ground, very close to Goldfield itself. The shaft was expertly timbered with axe-cut ironwood, in the Spanish manner. Lewis climbed down. At a depth of seventy-five feet, he found a lode of very rich ore. This could only be Peralta's mine.

Lewis formed a partnership with four friends and quickly removed $42,000 worth of gold before breaking into another larger and more modern shaft. This was believed to be part of Hall's shaft which had been displaced by the landslide. It seems, then, that Peralta had marked the relevant mountain with one boulder and had covered the shaft itself with another. Lewis and his partners could only conclude that the rest of their vein—the great mother lode—had been swept away by the flood. It is equally possible that it is now somewhere deep in the mountain or that it is as close to the surface as ever in a new position half a mile away. Our reference points must therefore be the two shafts.

Stolen Gold

I believe that we can profitably disregard Walz's directions and, indeed, Walz's whole story. It may be that he found some gold on Superstition, but it must be remembered that Walz had been dismissed from the Vulture Gold Mine at nearby Wickenburg, miles from Apache Junction, for 'high-grading', or stealing gold from the mine. A thorough search was made of the homes of the suspected miners, and some $175,000 worth of ore was retrieved. In Walz's cabin, though, not an ounce was found. He could not be prosecuted, but he was dismissed and the resentment of the imprisoned miners towards him is well recorded. If, as contemporary legend had it, Ken-tee had been spiriting large quantities of gold from the mine for him, he must have had a substantial hoard hidden away by the time that he settled near Superstition, in which case the resentment of those who suffered for his greed were well justified. Supposing that he had such a hoard, he could hardly dispatch it to the mint without explanation. He would undoubtedly have been hanged had he tried. Could it not be that, by his occasional trips to Superstition Mountain, Walz was using the popular legend to 'launder', as it were, his ill-gotten gains? The evidence is circumstantial, but it would explain many of the mysteries surrounding 'The Old Dutchman'— the ease with which he evaded pursuers, the sporadic nature of his trips to get further funds, the garbled and inaccurate directions that he left on his death, the speed with which, on his 'mining' trips, he returned with consistently high grade gold and the trivial but curious fact that, on his last trip to the Mountain, he returned with so small a quantity of gold.

FURTHER ACTION

With this site it is absurd to set any store by the various clues, many handed down from the most doubtful sources, and the same must be said of all the treasure maps. There is little chance of any more of the packsaddles turning up, and searchers are strongly advised to concentrate on Hall's lost mother lode. The use of electronic equipment is strongly recommended, of which details are given at the end of the account of Guadalupe de Tayopa.

The searcher should be aware that, for all its popularity, Superstition is still a hostile and dangerous sight. It is easier to stumble over a rattlesnake or a crumbling cliff-edge than a lump of gold ore, and on a summer's day, when the temperature does not drop below one hundred degrees, dehydration is the greatest enemy, whilst at night, particularly in winter, temperatures below zero are not uncommon.

TUAMOTU ARCHIPELAGO, FRENCH POLYNESIA, CENTRAL PACIFIC

THE CHURCH TREASURE OF PISCO

Amongst the soldiers in the Peruvian army fighting against Chile in the war of 1859–60 was a quartet of unsavoury rogues—an Englishman, an Irishman, a Spaniard, and an American—probably motivated to enlist solely in the hope of obtaining plunder. They succeeded beyond their dreams, for one of them learned from a renegade priest (one Father Matteo, it is said) of a vast treasure stored in the crypt of the church at Pisco, a town on the Peruvian coast. This treasure was guarded night and day, but they resolved at once upon its theft and worked out an ingenious plan. Having discharged themselves or deserted from the army, they signed on at Panama as crew members of a small schooner which would take them to Pisco.

Their object was to win the confidence of the priests who guarded the treasure. Two of them—Diego Alvarez, the sinister Spaniard who led them and the Irishman, Killorain—were Roman Catholics and soon became regular attenders at Mass. Having ingratiated themselves, they reported to the priests a rumour they claimed to have heard. The renegade priest, they said, was coming with a band of followers to steal the treasure.

These were troubled times and, in that they named the priest and revealed knowledge of the existence of the treasure which was, even in Pisco, a closely guarded secret, they convinced the priests and threw them into a panic. Now the plotters threw in their masterstroke: why not temporarily remove the treasure to a sister-church, until the trouble was past? The priests gratefully agreed. The treasure, attended by several priests, would be put aboard a vessel bound for Callao. The mercenaries kindly offered their services as guards.

And so within a few weeks of their arrival at Pisco, a small vessel named the *Bosun Bird*, laden with treasure, set sail from the town one autumn morning with the priests' heartfelt blessings. Once at sea, the few priests, the captain and remainder of the crew were quickly disposed of, leaving the four men undisputed possessors of their prize.

And what a prize! The inventory runs as follows:

14 tons gold ingots
7 great golden candlesticks, studded with jewels
38 long diamond necklaces
  A quantity of jewelled rings
  A quantity of jewelled bracelets
  A quantity of jewelled crucifixes
1 chest uncut stones (probably rubies)
1 chest Spanish doubloons
  Various other jewels and ornaments.

But now what were they to do in order to avert suspicion? The resourceful Alvarez proposed that they hide the hoard in some remote spot and then sail off to a point where they could scuttle the schooner, and claim that they were survivors of a shipwreck. It was decided that the hiding-place should be amongst the South Sea Islands and the 'shipwreck' off Australia. In December 1859, they reached Tahiti and took on much needed supplies. They cruised around amongst the islands and at last selected as their hiding-place a lonely little coral atoll in the Tuamotu group (also called Paumotu). The treasure was landed with

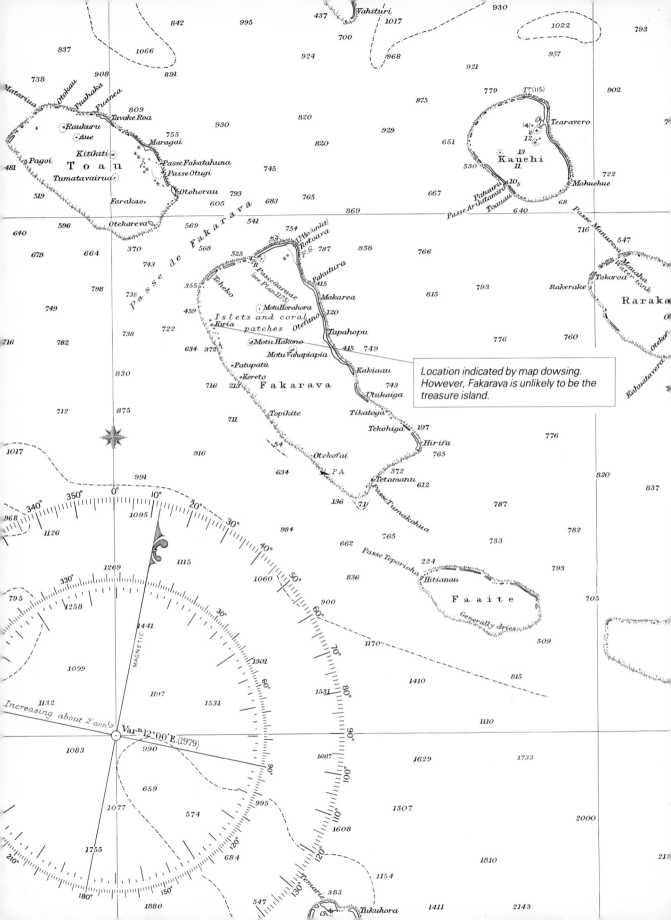

Location indicated by map dowsing. However, Fakarava is unlikely to be the treasure island.

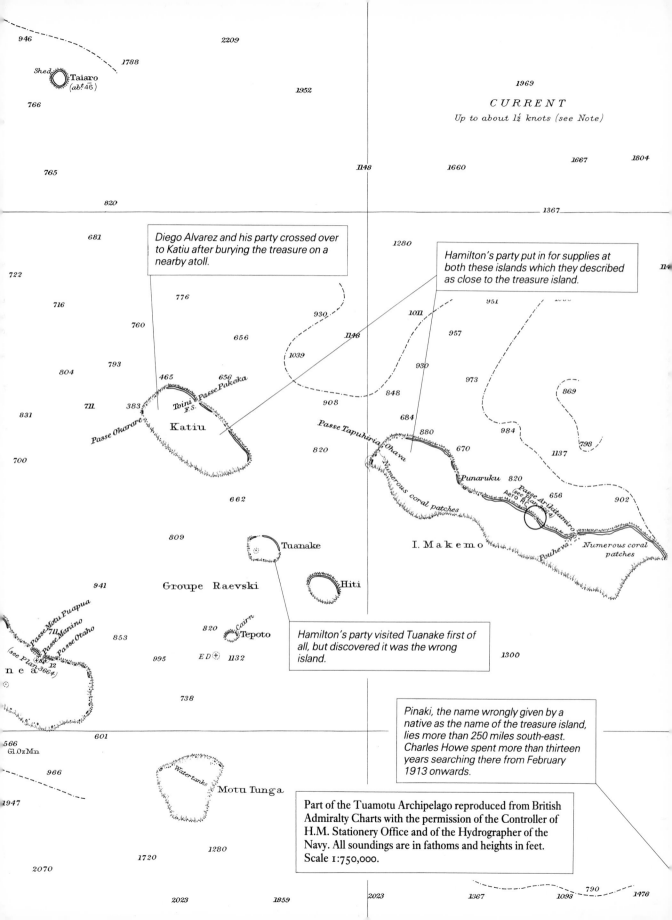

Diego Alvarez and his party crossed over to Katiu after burying the treasure on a nearby atoll.

Hamilton's party put in for supplies at both these islands which they described as close to the treasure island.

Hamilton's party visited Tuanake first of all, but discovered it was the wrong island.

Pinaki, the name wrongly given by a native as the name of the treasure island, lies more than 250 miles south-east. Charles Howe spent more than thirteen years searching there from February 1913 onwards.

Part of the Tuamotu Archipelago reproduced from British Admiralty Charts with the permission of the Controller of H.M. Stationery Office and of the Hydrographer of the Navy. All soundings are in fathoms and heights in feet. Scale 1:750,000.

great difficulty, for there was no harbour, and they had to transport everything, all 16 tons or so, in a small boat. For obvious reasons, therefore, the hiding-place can be assumed to be close to the water's edge.

After several weeks of hard work, the job was at last done. As Alvarez prepared a chart, he suddenly realized that, even after weeks of associating with the natives for supplies, he did not know the atoll's name.

They crossed over to nearby Katiu, but nothing quite happened as expected. They were told the name of an island, but, apparently, the wrong one: Pinaki. This error may have been partly due to the natives' lack of distinction between 'p' and 't'. Alvarez, believing he had the information he wanted, cold-bloodedly shot his informant. The story of this killing was well known in the islands in the 1930s.

After this ugly incident, the thieves had to leave hurriedly. In February, 1860, they scuttled their vessel near Cooktown, Australia, and on landing spun their yarn about a shipwreck. They had no trouble convincing their audience. They had brought a little gold from the treasure with them and lived quite happily for a while. But the last part of their plan was to return to reclaim the rest of the treasure, having now distanced themselves from their crimes. Their own means, however, were insufficient to fit out an expedition and they could not find any backers to believe their story of having acquired a treasure map.

They resolved to repair their fortunes in the Palmer gold fields. In a brush with natives, Alvarez and the Englishman of the party, Luke Barrett, were killed. Soon afterwards, Killorain and the American, Brown, were involved in a brawl which ended in a killing, for which both were sentenced to twenty years imprisonment: Brown died whilst serving his sentence.

In 1900 or thereabouts, the first attempt to remove the treasure seems to have been made: a man, called 'Luta' by the natives of Nukatavake, came and spent a month on Pinaki, presumably misled to that atoll by the original false indication of the native who was murdered. He searched and found nothing. Perhaps he was responsible for the curious signs on a block of coral near the atoll's centre.

Another man close to that date turned up in Tahiti claiming to be a descendant of Brown's. He is said to have come twice, first with companions in a boat fitted out for the recovery of the treasure. Carousing in Tahiti put paid to this first attempt, and the second, six years later, ended when he turned up with an *alias*, was identified to his face and stormed off in a rage leaving by the very ship on which he had come.

In May 1912 a former gold prospector, Charles Howe, received in his house near Sydney one rainy night a small and ancient tramp later described by him as 'altogether the most frightful-looking little dwarf that ever escaped out of a picture-book'. He was kind to this man and had his doubtful reward four months later when he was summoned to the tramp's bedside in a Sydney hospital. The dying man identified himself as Killorain, the last survivor of the quartet, now aged eighty-seven. Killorain gave him Alvarez' chart and made him promise to go in search of the treasure: he himself, said Killorain, had spent most of his life in prison since 1860 and had never been able to raise the funds to get back to the island. Howe gave his word and left the old man, meaning to return the following day; Killorain died three hours later.

Howe set about checking Killorain's story and was soon able to verify that there really had been a theft from Pisco and that four shipwrecked sailors had indeed landed near Cooktown in February 1860 from a ship called the *Bosun Bird*. Thoroughly convinced, he sold a small piece of property—all that he possessed—and booked his passage for Tahiti.

He reached it within a few months of Killorain's death and completed his unhappy journey to Pinaki in February 1913 where, in complete isolation, he built himself a small hut in the native style. Associating with the natives no further than necessity dictated, he systematically explored the atoll in search of the treasure.

Seven years after his arrival, the writer Charles Nordhoff was becalmed in a schooner less than a mile away and came ashore to visit him. Howe was frying some fish in front of his hut and welcomed him, though, in Nordhoff's words, 'a pair of the coldest blue eyes I have ever seen made me doubt the sincerity of it'. In fact, Howe proved friendly and talkative, perhaps starved more than he cared to admit of sympathetic companionship. But, though he talked freely of his past life, he never mentioned his mission on the island.

On the morning of the third windless day of Nordhoff's stay, he made an astonishing discovery while walking along the beach of the island's lagoon—a series of trenches on higher ground. 'I inspected the ditches under his guidance. There were three at least a quarter of a mile in length each and from three to four feet deep. These ran in parallel lines and were about four paces apart. Fifteen to twenty shorter trenches cut through them at right angles.' Howe told Nordhoff the story of the treasure, which he had thought he already knew.

That night the wind got up, and Nordhoff had no choice but to leave. In a brief farewell, he asked his host when he would consider leaving his lonely island. Howe replied that he would stay until he had found what he was looking for.

Poor Howe! For all his determination, Pinaki was none the less the wrong island. Some six years after Nordhoff's visit, he crossed over to Tahiti seeking enlightenment from the natives. In no time at all he was told the name of the deserted atoll which, tradition recorded, the *Bosun Bird* had actually visited.

Howe was off like a shot to the new atoll. All the important landmarks were there just as they were marked on his chart. There was the coral pinnacle on the eastern side, to the left of the pinnacle the pass into the lagoon, the pear-shaped pool, with seven coral blocks close by at even distances apart: this pool was supposed to hold the bulk of the treasure.

Howe expected to find two chests separate from the main cache in the pool. After three days' careful probing in the sand, his crow-bar struck against wood, and he brought to the surface the chest containing jewellery—a fabulous display of diamond necklaces, yards in length, uncut rubies piled high, jewel-studded golden candlesticks, and many other pieces.

His long quest was over. Another three days and he had found the chest full of doubloons. The contents of this chest, like those of the first, were transferred into a number of copra sacks and reburied.

Howe's final task was to search the pear-shaped pool containing the gold ingots. With a long probe he brought up from its depths a sliver of rotten oak, which satisfied him that the ingots were really there.

Howe's work was over for the time being. He would return to Tahiti, pretending that after all these years his quest was a failure. Then he would get a passage to Australia, raise money to charter a vessel, and return in secret to claim his prize.

It was four years after his return before he could find anyone prepared to risk his money, and further delays meant that an increasingly frustrated Howe was still waiting for something to happen in 1932. Howe decided to fill in his time with a little prospecting and left Sydney for the bush, with every intention of keeping in touch with his sponsors. After three letters received from him there was silence. Howe was never seen or heard of again, despite frantic efforts made to re-establish contact.

In January 1934, the expedition to which he should have been guide arrived in Tahiti. Six men made up the party including the diver, George Hamilton, to whose book on the expedition we owe our knowledge of events. They had permission from the authorities to search the Tuamotus but were still ignorant as to which particular one they should be investigating.

They had received various clues from Howe and latterly had obtained even Alvarez' chart from amongst Howe's private papers, but not the atoll's all-important name—or rather, no doubt by way of insurance for Howe, the *wrong* name.

At last, after a tour of several atolls, they found on one all the appropriate landmarks and Hamilton met on a neighbouring island a talkative native who confirmed Howe's former presence upon it. They had some measurements from Howe for locating some part of the treasure which were to be taken from the pinnacle—84 ft. E. by N., and 75 ft. N. by E. They dug a trench, some 12 ft. by 4 ft., at this designated spot and found nothing.

A little disheartened, they turned their attention to the pool, which was about 12 ft. deep, its floor covered by thick sand and broken coral. Hamilton dived, and at length succeeded in shifting all the coral but for one large block. Then he began drilling into the sand. At the

George Hamilton, the diver amongst the party of six who set out for the Tuamotu archipelago in January 1934. They found the correct atoll without difficulty but their problems were only just beginning. Confrontations with an octopus and a giant moray eel nearly cost Hamilton his life.

This coffer-dam, built out of sheets of corrugated iron, was designed by Hamilton's party to prevent sand returning into the hole they were digging at the bottom of the pear-shaped pool believed to contain the major part of the Pisco treasure. Unfortunately, the sand still managed to penetrate underneath and the dam's failure marked the end of their attempt.

Although the name of the atoll where the Pisco treasure lies hidden has been kept secret, these photographs exist of the pear-shaped pool, where most of the searching was done. The wooden arms of the coffer-dam seen in the right-hand picture are supposed to be directly over the treasure.

sixth attempt and 6 ft. into the sand, his drill struck something that was neither sand nor rock. Delighted as he was, he saw that digging in the normal way was impossible, as the hole would fill up with sand too quickly.

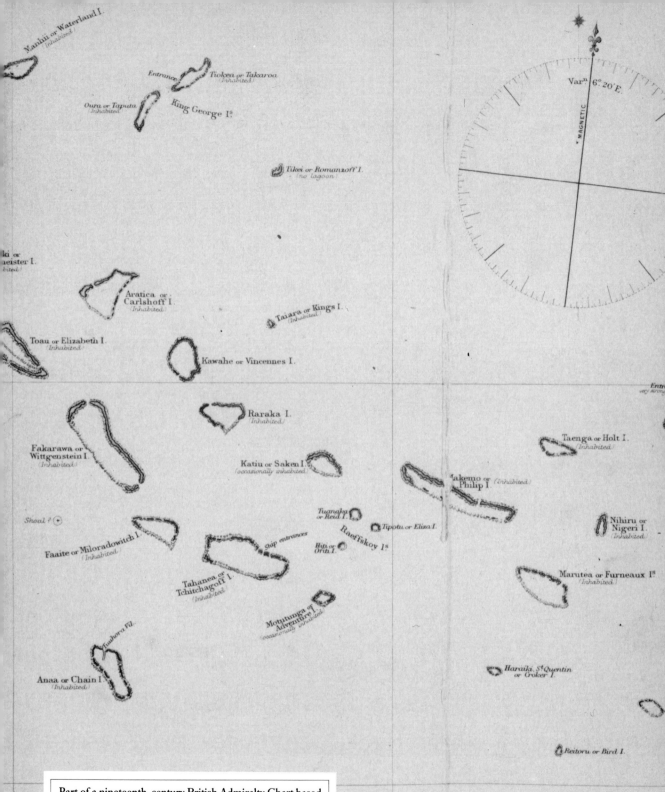

Manhii or Waterland I.
(Inhabited)

Entrance
Tiokea or Takaroa
Inhabited

Oura or Taputa
Inhabited
King George Is.

Tikei or Romanzoff I.
(no lagoon)

Varⁿ 6°. 20'E.

MAGNETIC

ki or
aeister I.
bited

Aratica or
Carlshoff I.
Inhabited

Taiara or Kings I.
Inhabited

Toau or Elizabeth I.
(Inhabited)

Kawahe or Vincennes I.

Raraka I.
(Inhabited)

Entran
g along th

Fakarawa or
Wittgenstein I.
(Inhabited)

Katiu or Saken I.
(occasionally inhabited)

Taenga or Holt I.
(Inhabited)

Makemo or
Philip I. *(Inhabited)*

Shoal? ⊙

Tuanaka
or Reid I.
Tipotu or Eliza I.
Raeffskoy Is.

Nihiru or
Nigeri I.
(Inhabited)

Faaite or Miloradowitch I.
(Inhabited)

Ship entrances
Hiti or
Ofiti I.

Tahanea or
Tchitchagoff I.
(Inhabited)

Marutea or Furneaux Is.
(Inhabited)

Motuhunga or
Adventure I.
(occasionally inhabited)

mahora Vil

Anaa or Chain I.
(Inhabited)

Haraiki St Quentin
or Groïer I.

H

Reitoru or Bird I.

 Buyers Group
F.D.
*Sought for in vain by
Lieut. Parchappe in 1855*

It was agreed that they should build a coffer-dam out of sheets of corrugated iron so as to prevent sand dug out of the hole from returning. This was easily put together and Hamilton was underwater, lowering it into position when he felt a sharp jerk on his ankle. He turned around to find himself staring at a huge octopus. He jabbed with his knife at the tentacle which gripped him, and managed to break free. He shot to the surface amid a cloud of blood and ink.

After this incident, Hamilton learned to be respectful of the pool's tidal movements (it was fed by the lagoon) and mostly went down in the company of a native diver, Vigo. It was Vigo who spotted when they were both down there the biggest moray eel Hamilton had ever seen: Moray eels are fearless and vicious and will attack a man without hesitation. They are—or were at that time—responsible for many deaths amongst the pearl-divers. The two divers fled upwards to enjoy a second narrow escape.

It took them some time to realize that the coffer-dam was not working. Sand was still coming in underneath. They saw that they would need proper equipment and resolved to go back to Tahiti to await further money from London, as their finances were almost exhausted.

Without knowing it, they had shot their bolt. The London end of the expedition was involved in an expensive libel action, from which the syndicate was eventually exonerated after the damage had been done. The expedition was obliged to return home for lack of funds.

FURTHER ACTION

Pinaki has been searched periodically. Pinaki, however, is not the treasure atoll, nor for that matter is Tuanake, the atoll which Hamilton's party first visited. Alvarez and his accomplices never knew the name, Howe knew it latterly but never told anyone, and Hamilton's party never revealed it. Recently it has been identified with Fakarava, but this is a large and inhabited island and was so in Alvarez's day. The correct island will be one that is small, was uninhabited at that time and is near to Katiu and Makemo, at both of which Hamilton's party put in for supplies. Study of the illustrated French chart, which is almost contemporary with the burial of the treasure, reveals a choice of several islands. The correct one will have the relevant landmarks:

1. A coral pinnacle on the eastern side.
2. A pass just to the left of the pinnacle.
3. A pear-shaped pool, with seven coral blocks nearby, about three miles from the pass.

In addition, we know that there is a tremendous surf by the reef, though this is common among the atolls, and no anchorage or entry into the lagoon for a schooner. From Tuanake, the treasure atoll was the third that Hamilton's party visited. It will not take an earnest seeker long to find. Hamilton's party, at the same disadvantage as we are, took one day to find it.

The contents of the two chests Howe discovered, which he re-buried when he left the atoll, are most likely to be buried at a depth of only a few feet. This is the sort of search ideal for even the most basic model of metal detector, for the treasure will be packed together or spread over a very small area in the event that the sacks to which it was transferred have rotted away. There are unlikely to be other metal objects in the vicinity that will hamper the search.

The gold ingots in the pear-shaped pool present a whole set of problems requiring small-scale engineering work ...

Further information can be found in Nordhoff's *Faery Lands of the South Seas* and George Hamilton's *Treasure of the Tuamotus*. Neither, it should be said, is entirely to be trusted as to detail.

INDEX

159